D0191192

PLANNING YOUR CAREER IN ASSOCIATION MANAGEMENT

Paul A. Belford

WASHINGTON, DC

Information in this book is accurate as of the time of publication and consistent with standards of good practice in the general management community. As research and practice advance, however, standards may change. For this reason, it is recommended that readers evaluate the applicability of any recommendation in light of particular situations and changing standards.

American Society of Association Executives
1575 I Street, NW
Washington, DC 20005-1103
Phone: (888) 950-2723
Fax: (202) 408-9634
E-mail: books@asaenet.org

ASAE's core purpose is to advance the value of voluntary associations to society and to support the professionalism of the individuals who lead them.

Susan Robertson, Vice President, Marketing and Communications
Anna Nunan, Director of Book Publishing
Louise Quinn, Acquisitions Coordinator
Jennifer Moon, Production Manager
Anthony Conley, Operations Coordinator
Edited by Sandra R. Sabo

Cover design by John Hubbard and interior design by Northeastern Graphic Services

This book is available at a special discount when ordered in bulk quantities. For information, contact the ASAE Member Service Center at (202) 371-0940.

A complete catalog of titles is available on the ASAE Web site at www.asaenet.org/bookstore

Printed in the United States of America.

10 9 8 7 6 5 4 3 2 1

Contents

PART II: TAKING COMMAND

Acknowledgments

To my friends and associates who helped me in the development and preparation of this book, I am sincerely grateful. I am also greatly indebted to client search committees and executives whose insights, trust, and openness have been instrumental to the success of the searches conducted and to the development of many of the ideas and views that follow.

Although listing names risks leaving out others who were helpful and supportive, I would like to thank Jill Cornish, publisher of *Association Trends,* for her encouragement to write on association staffing issues and the following for their assistance and encouragement in reviewing the manuscript: Bob Angle, former Executive Vice President, Building Owners and Managers Association; Jerry Connors, President, Data Interchange Standards Association; Jim Cramer, former Executive Vice President, American Institute of Architects; Steve Fellman, Partner, Galland, Khrasch; Bill Good, CAE, Executive Vice President, National Roofing Contractors Association; Jerry Jacobs, Partner, Shaw Pittman; Pamela Kaul, President, Association Strategies; George Koch, former President, Grocery Manufacturers of America; Peter McCarthy, President, McCarthy and Company; and Steve McConnell, Senior Vice President for Public Policy, the Alzheimer's Association. I would like to extend a special thanks to Don DeBolt, President, International Franchise Association, a good friend and professional associate whose insights, counsel, and encouragement were invaluable to the completion of the project.

To say that the book could not have been completed without the assistance of ASAE staff is to state the obvious. However, I would like to thank Anna Nunan, Director of Book Publishing, for her support, and especially

Louise Quinn, Acquisitions Coordinator, whose cooperative spirit and easy availability lightened the load and speeded the process. I am particularly indebted to ASAE President and CEO, Mike Olson, CAE, whose encouragement to undertake the project provided the incentive needed to begin it.

I would also like to thank Joe DeGioia, President, JDG Associates, for his support, and Mary Bentz, for her assistance in the preparation of the final manuscript as well as for her contribution to the development and growth of JDG's association search practice.

Finally, I would like to thank my wife, Michaele Anne, whose support and encouragement in this and all that I do is invaluable and greatly appreciated.

About
the Author

Paul A. Belford, principal, JDG Associates Ltd., Rockville, Maryland, has been a professional search consultant with a specialty in association executive search since 1990. Other areas of search include the related fields of government relations and communications.

Prior to his career in executive search, Paul spent 11 years with Pharmaceutical Research and Manufacturers of America (PhRMA), a major Washington D.C.-based trade association, where he was responsible for international issues management. Previous to PhRMA, he served 12 years with the United States government, most of which was in the Office of the Assistant Secretary for International Affairs at the Treasury Department.

Paul holds a bachelor's degree in accounting from Boston College and a master's in economics from Fordham University.

Introduction

The content of this book is based on 11 years in senior management at a national trade association and more than a decade as an executive recruiter specializing in association executive placement. In the course of conducting more than 100 chief executive officer (CEO) and senior management searches for clients ranging from national trade and professional associations to regional and state organizations, I have seen certain patterns and trends emerge in terms of what works and what does not.

But career building is not an exact science, if a science at all. There are few hard and fast rules. Career building depends upon judgment and commitment, with some guessing and luck thrown in for good measure.

Planning Your Career in Association Management was written for both association professionals and for those who are considering a career in the association field. Chapters are designed to be read separately, independent of what precedes or follows. Accordingly, you will find several cross-references to other chapters throughout the text.

The book is divided into two parts. *Part I: Taking Charge* outlines a career-development process that you initiate and control. In other words, a career in associations doesn't just happen: You make it happen. This section covers basic information, such as career tracking, the association environment, writing a resume, and conducting a job search in the association industry. *Part II: Taking Command* focuses on fulfilling the role of a chief executive officer. Even if your goal is not to become a CEO, you'll find valuable information on topics such as working with executive recruiters and evaluating what an association has to offer—and what you can offer in return.

A Unique Environment

In my work as an association professional, as an executive recruiter, and in interviews with hundreds of association professionals each year, I have discerned an association persona—the type of person who succeeds in association work. It is: *A person who is able to take professional fulfillment from group achievement.*

If this does not describe you—if you are uncomfortable with such an environment—you may want to look elsewhere to build a career. In fact, you should. You can never own an association. When you work for one, you work for those who *do* own it—the members and the leaders who volunteer their time to advance the common interests of their industry or profession. Associations have a culture of giving and sharing in the achievement and advancement of common goals. It is what makes them unique.

There is compensation beyond the paycheck, however. Truth be told, there's a type of ownership as well. As an association professional, you are at the nexus of a profession or industry, the place where all the forces meet whether on a critical issue or a national convention or the emergence of a new product or service. Associations forge change; that is why many of them were established. You can become part of an industry or a profession, helping it work better and grow stronger. True, you can't sell that on the NASDAQ, but you keep that experience with you wherever you go.

Paul A. Belford
Kensington, Maryland
August 2001

PART I

TAKING
CHARGE

CHAPTER 1

Career Tracking

How many times have you encountered someone who shrugged and said, "My career in associations has really been a fluke. I didn't have a clue what I'd end up doing"? It doesn't have to be that way.

Reduced to its simplest form, career tracking means that your career is something that you do rather than something that happens to you. Ideally, you end up where you wanted to be before you got there, rather than some place where time and fate deposited you. It means continually evaluating what you do well, discovering what you like to do, developing new skills, and discovering with whom and for whom you want to work, all in the context of situations you either encounter by chance or seek out on purpose. Career tracking is only for those to whom professional fulfillment and personal growth are non-negotiable goals and objectives. It requires taking a leadership role in your life and adding value to the organizations or circumstances in which you find yourself.

Career tracking is *not* office politics and manipulation, working the angles and weaknesses of others to your advantage. Rather, it involves focusing first on the success of the organization and, second, on your improving your ability to bring value to the organization and assuming an active role in that success.

A successful career involves two winners: you and the organization for which you work. In the days of sailing ships, when sailors climbed tall masts in a full gale to shorten sail, there was a rule: "One hand for yourself and one hand for the ship." While the contemporary office environment is hardly as hazardous as edging out on a yardarm over a surging sea, the relationship is the same—one of mutual benefit and mutual dependence.

Line Versus Staff

In an association environment, career tracking begins with an awareness and understanding of the field and its elements and your ability to locate yourself within it, both now and in the future. Some elements of career tracking apply to all organizations, whether nonprofit or for-profit. The first is understanding the distinction between "line" and "staff" positions. A line function is one that the organization was established to perform; a staff function is one performed so that the line function can be realized.

As an example, consider the management of the assembly line versus the management of the accounting function in an automobile company. For the company to succeed, both functions must be performed well. Yet, the company was not established to count numbers but to manufacture cars, so the manager of the assembly line is in a *line* function and the manager of the accounting department is in a *staff* function.

In the universe of associations, it is possible for the same activity to be line in one organization and staff in another. Take public affairs in the widget industry. A person doing public affairs at a widget company is in a staff position—that is, the company was not established to do public affairs but to make widgets. But serving as public affairs director for the National Widget Association is a line activity because the association was established precisely to do public affairs for the industry.

Knowing whether you are in a staff or a line function is essential, because it is highly unusual in the association field for a professional in a staff activity to move into a leadership position. Thus, the head of an association's finance and administration function is unlikely to be tapped to serve as the CEO. Not impossible, mind you—but highly unlikely. Moreover, not every line position is necessarily a direct route to the executive suite. Among the three or four line functions in an association (typically conventions/meetings, government relations, training/education, and public affairs), one or two are viewed as most important by the lion's share of the members. Not surprisingly, those on senior staff heading these functions are the more likely to be tapped to succeed a departing CEO should the volunteer leadership look inside for a successor.

Issues Versus Services

Within the line functions, the focus will either be on issues or services. An issues-driven organization focuses primarily on advocacy and lobbying. Its members look to it for representation in different forums and before official bodies, such as Congress, state legislatures, or regulatory agencies. They also want the association to promote the members' function within an industrial community (for example, the distributor segment of the widget industry). A services-driven association focuses primarily on providing member services, such as group insurance plans, training, credentialing, an annual convention with a trade show/exhibit, networking, publications (magazines, journals, newsletters), and a Web site. In addition, some associations were established to provide a service that the market could not, such as the setting of standards for a profession or an industry.

Association professionals who work in the issues area typically have political science, government, or other social-science degrees and are likely to have worked in a legislative or regulatory environment, a consulting firm, a think tank, or academia. They are generally more motivated by concepts and causes and are comfortable dealing with broad activities that affect the environment in which their members operate, either as private corporations or individuals in a professional practice or other career line.

Those on the services side frequently come from the area of service—for example, a convention management company, a publishing house, an insurance agency, or an information-technology firm. Their academic degrees are often of a technical or functional nature, such as marketing, general business, or computer science. Also, it is not uncommon for an association careerist to have entered the field as a generalist and have developed an expertise in a particular area, such as membership development.

Professional Development Versus Career Advancement

Career tracking is not solely a get-to-the-top-of-the-heap activity. Over the course of a career, you may move in and out of concentrating on what you do (a discipline, such as government relations or convention management) versus where you are in the organization (director, vice president, president). Many professionals in the association world do not aspire to become the CEO. You might, for instance, wish to pursue a career in certification, convention management, or chapter relations. Career tracking involves knowing what you want to do and being certain that you will be in a position to do it—and to get better at it. (See Chapter 2.)

Staying Ahead

Let's examine the risks of being in a line function whose importance to the membership is on the decline. Say you are the assistant vice president for

Finding a Mentor

Webster's College Dictionary defines a mentor as "a wise and trusted counselor or teacher." This person might be a half generation or more older who has succeeded in the field, has a genuine interest in you personally, and is happy to share what he or she has learned. Developing a relationship with such a person, even if it means just conversing over lunch or coffee several times a year, can help you take stock of your career and even the rest of your life.

While good mentors provide comfort in times of disappointment and dispense the occasional pearl of wisdom, they are most useful in helping you listen to yourself. Rather than telling you about themselves, good mentors tell you what you are telling them—but are not listening to yourself. They help you focus—perhaps even uncover—your hopes, dreams, goals, and aspirations.

If you'd like to develop a mentoring relationship, look for:

- A professional with whom you may have worked at an earlier stage in your career, whose advice and counsel you sought in the past.
- A person who takes a genuine interest in the professional development and well-being of others and has the self-confidence to share what he or she has learned with others.
- Someone whose character and reputation is built on achievement rather than celebrity, who engenders the friendship and confidence of his or her peers.
- Someone who has the time and proximity to meet with you several times a year without it being a burden or imposition.
- A professional whose company you enjoy—a friend or a person you would like to be, not someone you feel any need to impress.

government affairs in an association that is shifting from an issues orientation to a services orientation. The most obvious risk is in the compensation area: The larger raises are likely to favor those who perform the functions the members see as most important to their interests. Your ability to make a difference, both within and outside the association, will probably decrease as the focus on services increases. This is not simply a matter of hubris or ego. The lower profile you have in your organization, the less professional fulfillment will be available to you in contributing to its success and growth. Also, as a function's importance declines, the association as a platform for professional development declines with it.

Play out the scenario further. As your association loses interest—and influence—in an issue, invitations to lead or join coalitions will decline. As your exposure to groups at the cutting edge of an issue diminishes, the more difficult it will be to find professional fulfillment. When professional development stalls, so does career advancement. To get back on track, you may have to find a new position with another organization.

In fact, shifting from one organization to another has been standard practice for association professionals; your career may include positions with as many as six different organizations. Job changes will only be accelerated by economic forces and management trends, such as outsourcing, technological advances, consolidations and mergers of associations or their members, and the creation of new associations around emerging industries. Moving every three years or so, especially at the beginning of a career, is not

---

Risk Management

Moving from one association to another bears with it many risks. Chief among these is poor judgment. The desire to serve as chief executive officer frequently contributes to a bad decision: taking a new position primarily because of its title, without adequate regard to whether it is a good fit with your talents, personality, and ability to serve.

Take, for example, the vice president of government affairs at a large, high-tech association whose members were all Fortune 500 firms and whose issues were discussed weekly in the national and business press. This professional's desire (call it an itch) to be a CEO resulted in his accepting a position as head of a low-tech industry association whose members were largely small companies and whose leadership was composed of second- and third-generation family executives. Moreover, it was a highly services-oriented group with few issues that ever made the national press. The change in cultures was significant. Though successful in the position, the executive wanted out after three months; it took another 18 months before he returned to a high-tech association offering a better fit and professional fulfillment.

The CEO itch has other manifestations, such as moving from a national to a state association "to get CEO experience." The expectation is that the next move will be to a CEO position at the national level. While this route can succeed, search committees of national associations generally look past state-level executives when seeking candidates. Their strong preference is likely for an executive who is already serving as a national CEO or as a senior executive in a national association.

If, therefore, you have your sights set on a national CEO position, consider service as a CEO at the state level, move to a national organization in a senior executive position, and then move to a national CEO position. Nothing is sure in life, least of all tracks to becoming an association CEO, but it helps to learn the probabilities.

Getting on Track

Spend some time answering these 12 questions truthfully, and you'll have a good start on career tracking.

1. Am I in a line or staff position?
2. Is my organization issues- or services-driven?
3. Am I in an issues or services position?
4. How important is what my organization does to its members? How important was it to its members three years ago? How important will it be three years from now?
5. Am I perceived by the members with whom I work as important to the success of the organization?
6. Do I believe that the position I am in (line/staff or issues/services) is one in which I will be able to continue to grow professionally?
7. Would I like my supervisor's job? Am I prepared to serve in it should I be offered it?
8. Where in this organization would I like to be in five years?
9. Who in this organization do I admire most?
10. Of all the professionals with whom I work inside or outside the organization, whom do I admire most?
11. What are my chances of ever serving in his or her position? Can I get there from here?
12. Do I have a mentor? Who would I like my mentor to be? Who would like to be my mentor?

"job hopping," provided you are growing as a professional in each position and are increasingly adding value to the organizations for which you work. A professional who moves from one position to successively better positions, especially if recruited from one to the other, is someone to watch. As a career progresses, of course, the time spent in each position can be expected to lengthen. The principle, however, remains the same: You must be of value to the organization, and the organization must be of value to you.

CHAPTER 2

Discipline, Management, and Leadership

The story is as American as apple pie. You start at the bottom, say as the meetings coordinator. You work hard and keep learning, and the association promotes you to director of meetings. Then you enter the ranks of management, first as a vice president and then maybe chief operating officer. Next you become a chief executive officer and, after numerous farewell parties, you retire at 65, a wise person who is respected by one and all. Simple, right?

Well, nothing is that simple, especially the ladder to the top, or even to the middle. In fact, it's not even a ladder, where each step is seen from the one below. A career is more like a maze, complete with trap doors and blind alleys. The maze has rules, however. The first rule is persistence: Keep going. And the second rule? The only way to succeed is by following the first rule. Roles, structures, missions, and parameters change as outside forces affect organizations internally and externally. Knowing the dynamics of organizations and where the decision points are likely to occur in careers is useful.

Here are three terms whose definitions will help you **navigate** the career maze:

- *Discipline:* A skill or an expertise that conforms to certain standards of practice and is viewed as transferable from one employment situation to another. The more rigorous disciplines include medicine, law, and accounting. Disciplines common to the association profession include public affairs, meeting planning, human resources, education, and publishing, to name a few. Credentials (for example, Certified Meeting Planner) are generally available and strengthen a person's ability to serve in a specific area.

- *Management:* Supervising the activities of others, including those with professional disciplines, in the achievement of a directed goal or objective.

- *Leadership:* Providing direction and support to the management level; identifying the goals and objectives, ensuring the resources to achieve the goals are available, and motivating and holding accountable those to whom the resources are provided.

The Box Score

Assume you are 24 years old, a year or two out of college. You have had a few jobs and, after responding to a classified ad, now find yourself the meetings coordinator at the American Widget Association (AWA). While happy and enthusiastic about your new job, you know you are at the bottom of the organization chart handed to you during employee orientation. You assume, quite reasonably, that the organization resembles a pyramid-shaped triangle (Figure 1). At the top of the pyramid is the CEO, with the Number Two (chief operating officer) just beneath, and so forth . . .

STOP! It's not a pyramid. It's really a box. The CEO drew the pyramid and, from where he or she sits, that figure is an apt depiction of the organization. But you are not a CEO, and this is not an organizational manage-

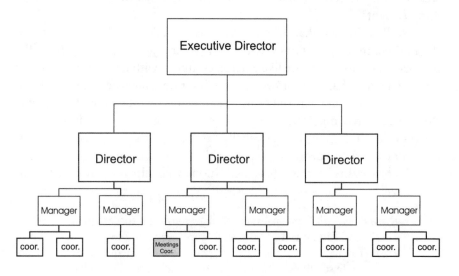

FIGURE 1

ment course. This is a career-development discussion, and the most important person on that chart is Y-O-U. We are not talking about how AWA operates but about what happens to you from now on.

What's the difference between the box and the organizational pyramid? The pyramid is designed to express the relationships among the professionals within an organization, each with specific disciplines, whose energies are directed at designated tasks that contribute to the overall mission of the association. It is static and created to promote the goals of the organization without particular regard to the career interests of those depicted on it. On the other hand, the box (Figure 2) depicts the growth prospects of someone who starts at a particular place and, over time, has the potential to grow in four dimensions: discipline, management, leadership, and the type of employer.

As shown in Figure 2, the meetings coordinator starts at the novice level and eventually masters the discipline of meetings management. Opportunities at the management level then emerge in the two types of organizations: a meetings management company and an association. In the association, this move could mean becoming the meetings manager or director, with responsibility for supervising the meetings department and its five employees. In the company, moving up could mean heading a team or division with responsibility for four annual meetings, two of which might have a trade show.

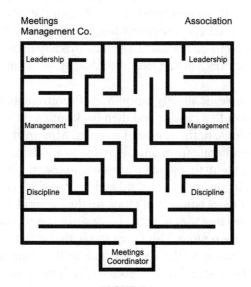

FIGURE 2

Regardless of the type of organization, success during the early stages of management would likely lead to greater management responsibility. The association professional might take on the supervision of the education and training departments, as well as the meetings department. In the meetings company, added responsibility might mean tripling the number of shows supervised, plus oversight of larger, more prestigious events, with business development responsibility as well. At this level, career possibilities begin to narrow. For the association professional, the discipline shifts from specific meetings management to the more general supervision of professionals in a number of disciplines (meetings, education, and so forth), each of whom should be expected to know as much as or more than the manager about each discipline. By contrast, the meetings company professional remains in the meetings discipline. This professional's relative strength in the discipline will determine the competitiveness of the company.

At the leadership level, the differences are even more pronounced. The association CEO will routinely be an executive with the demonstrated ability to manage an array of tasks. His or her primary responsibility is to help volunteer leaders determine the mission and direction of the association, translate this perspective into an operational plan, and then execute the plan. The company CEO's responsibilities include ensuring that the company can deliver a good product or service and developing relationships with association CEOs and other potential clients to win service contracts. The core competency of the CEO is in delivering meetings services; the company measures its success largely by the amount of profit it earns annually. The association CEO's core competency is in relationship development and enhancement. His or her success is measured by membership satisfaction across a wide range of services, including those of meetings management.

This, of course, is greatly simplified. Professionals routinely move from an association to a vendor and then back, and within association and vendor organizations, in the course of a career. Moreover, those within the association might migrate from one discipline to another, for example from meetings management to membership development. That is exactly the point of the box. If you are 24 years old and the meetings coordinator of the American Widget Association, don't look up the pyramid. Look around and across the box—because the chances of ever sitting on top of the pyramid in this organization are remote. This is not to say that it can't happen. But going from the mailroom to the CEO's office in the same association happened rarely in the past and seems less likely to happen now.

Professional Credentials

Association professionals can earn a number of professional credentials. They include the Certified Association Executive (CAE) designation offered by the American Society of Association Executives, the Certified Meeting Planner (CMP) from the Meeting Professionals International, the Certified Fund Raising Executive (CFRE) from the Association of Fundraising Professionals, and Accredited in Public Relations (APR) from the Public Relations Society of America. Most of these require a demonstration of expertise, including a written examination.

Should you make the effort to earn a professional credential? The answer depends on how long you intend to stay in the discipline or an area related to it and whether you have the time and resources to invest. Earning a specific credential does not lock you into the discipline track rather than the association track. It means that if you are in a position that is likely to last for three years or so—and you enjoy doing it—you have decided to learn more about the discipline from people who are experts. In addition to what you learn, participating in a structured program will put you in the company of others of similar interests. These colleagues may not only enrich your life professionally but also prove to be valuable contacts as you build your career. There is, in fact, something of a natural selection process at play in pursuing a professional credential. In doing so, you join others who are taking an extra step to grow professionally and take charge of their careers.

If you plan to build a career in associations, earning a credential is advisable if for no other reason than professional development and credentialing are among the missions of most associations. Earning a credential in your field of work will enhance your ability to perform and add value in your current position, enhance your professional fulfillment, and possibly strengthen your ability to land a better position in the future.

For instance, to an executive recruiter, a CAE designation means that the candidate knows what associations are, what they do, and how they interrelate with one another. The credential increases the probability that the candidate can manage well and understands the dynamics of staff and membership in operating an association. The CAE also indicates that the candidate has a high regard for what associations do and has made a commitment to grow professionally.

In addition, search committees often favor candidates who have earned the CAE designation. For a professional society, especially one that offers a credential, it indicates a commitment to career development and growth, as well as a firsthand appreciation of what an association can offer to its members. In fact, search committees of professional societies often show little interest in candidates who may have 20 years' experience in associations but haven't earned the association field's professional credential. In short, credentialing is where the winners are.

A Game Plan

Accordingly, you should focus on finding comfort and interest in the job you currently have and then get better at it, becoming of increasing value to the organization. As you improve and are recognized by those who work with and above you, be alert to opportunities in management as they present themselves, if you are so inclined. Remember, though, some people choose to focus on their discipline and leave the management function to others. Many with this inclination join neither association nor company but become independent consultants. As such, they can concentrate on a particular skill area, become recognized as experts, and provide services in that area to a range of clients.

If you wish to take the first step into management, be aware that it may not be in the association where you began, or even in an association. In the example above, you might work for a meetings management company or perhaps a hotel property or chain. That's why, in the early stages of your working life, you should forget about the top of the pyramid and look at the discipline you are in and what lies just next to or above it. Associations measure success by membership satisfaction; companies look at the bottom line. You should measure success by professional fulfillment, which is a continuing process throughout your working life.

Winning is not necessarily getting to the top of the pyramid. Winning is playing hard and well and smart. Keep that in mind, and you'll be in charge of your career and will greatly enhance the part of your life spent at work.

CHAPTER 3

The Association Setting

Association management is not a career that new graduates routinely seek out or are even aware of. While association disciplines have become more demanding and appear to be attracting professionals at a younger age, a wide range of opportunities exists for those entering at mid-career. In fact, mid-career entry is common in the association profession.

If you are newly graduated or at mid-career, here are the unique aspects of the environment in which most trade associations and professional societies operate.

Service

Associations are not created by staff. They are created by members who, for reasons of common interest, have banded together as a group. As the administrative and organizational burdens of the association become more than the volunteer members can manage on their own, they hire paid staff to help them.

This is the origin of association management as a profession, and so it remains today. The role of the association professional is to help and assist those who created and support the association, those who give it purpose and direction toward the achievement of its goals. The role of a trade association is not to make a better widget, but to make the world a better place for those who make widgets.

Consensus

Consensus is how associations come into being, how they operate, and the purpose for their existence. In associations, consensus development is synonymous with decision making. For the association professional, there can be no more important a task than helping members come to consensus on as wide a range of issues as possible. (See Chapter 8.)

Consensus development—which is often compared to herding cats—requires exceptional communication skills, with an emphasis on the *listening* half of the communication function, and patience. More important is the need to have a generosity of spirit. Association professionals willingly forgo credit for success and are at ease with assigning the credit to someone else—perhaps even the person who was most reluctant to join in the consensus.

Policy and Execution

The members, through the board of directors, set an association's policy and direction. Staff contribute to this activity as the board sees appropriate; each association has its own culture and view on this issue. Once the policy and direction are set, staff has responsibility for policy execution and goal achievement. Here again, each association has its own culture regarding the degree to which volunteers play a role in policy execution and implementation. Understanding this culture—and being comfortable with it—is critical.

Culture

While all organizations have cultures reflecting their mode of operation, associations are unique in having a culture that reflects the relationship between members and staff. Culture is often expressed in terms of how "member driven" the association is. By definition, all associations are member-driven because they are owned by the members; if the members did not "drive" the association, it would lose direction and purpose and eventually dissolve. Just *how* member-driven any particular association may be depends on a wide range of variables.

A good measure of the degree to which an association is member-driven is the level of staff participation in the development of a strategic plan. For example, if the staff plays a secretarial role in the development of a strategic plan, with only the CEO attending the meetings (but not actively participating or contributing), the association would be viewed as highly member-driven. Conversely, if the staff is asked to provide input, and senior staff, along with the CEO, contribute to the plan's development, the association would be seen as less member-driven, perhaps approaching a partnership between board and staff.

While many associations have gradually shifted toward a partnership model between board and staff, there is no "wrong" culture. Certainly, staff should try to influence and affect the association's culture should it start taking the group away from fulfilling the needs of the members. This is, in fact, a major responsibility of the professional association manager. At the end of the day, however, an association's culture will (and should) reflect that of the membership and the members' views on the association's role and purpose.

Compared to private-sector corporations, associations have no specific test on profit, cash flow, or return on investment. While an association's annual surpluses and membership levels, trade-show revenues, and legislative victories all play a role in a chief executive officer's annual review, member satisfaction is the ultimate measure of success. This is frequently reflective of the association's culture and not easily reducible to quantifiable measure.

Ownership

Another relationship unique to the association field is that of ownership: The customer is the owner. Although not all customers of an association are its members, the great majority of those who use, subscribe to, or purchase an association's products and services are members, and they have a distinct sense of ownership. This is especially true in a professional society or in a trade association with many members that are not large companies. The sense of ownership may vary among members, but one certainty remains: The staff never owns the association.

In a sense, this relationship puts association management ahead of the curve in management theory and practice. Associations have traditionally treated their "customers" as stakeholders, a relatively new concept for many for-profit organizations. The downside comes when the customer is wrong. As the experienced association professional knows, the difference between a dissatisfied customer who will not come back and the dissatisfied owner who will not leave is *huge*. Managing differences with the customer/owner calls for tact and diplomacy and sometimes courage. Here, as elsewhere in association management, the key word is service. Successful association professionals see themselves as being in service to the members and the profession or industry. Maintaining this attitude enables you to work through just about any situation that arises.

Association executives can have ownership in their associations. It comes from a commitment and dedication to the association's goals and objectives, what it and the industry or discipline it represents stands for. Although far less tangible than the common stock of a corporation, this can be a source of great personal fulfillment.

Members as Assets

Even though they are clearly owners of the organization, members should still be viewed as assets. The members, through the board, set direction and the staff executes it, but the execution of a policy or direction can clearly include a role for the members. Examples abound: testifying before official bodies; meeting with the media; providing access to policy makers, opinion leaders, and keynote speakers; and serving on seminar panels and education programs.

One key measure of the successful association professional is his or her ability to identify and engage key members in the activities of the association. This requires patience and a willingness to reach out and engage the membership, to learn and to understand their specific needs, and to know them as individuals.

Staff Liaisons

Mid-career entry is frequently at the director level or higher. This often means serving as a staff liaison for one or more association committees. As a staff liaison, an association professional has structured and direct contact with the membership and ventures beyond the organization chart. While still reporting to his or her supervisor within the association's staff structure, the staff liaison has another supervisor in the committee chair. And it is not uncommon for the two "bosses" to have different views on the committee's work or even its purpose. Tact is essential in such situations, which brings to mind a practical definition of diplomacy: letting the other person have it your way.

A committee staff liaison serves many roles, ranging from secretary to committee meetings (including drafting agendas, taking notes, and distributing materials) to facilitator of consensus, issues monitor, confidential advisor to the chair, and advocate of the committee's work. In fact, a committee is not unlike an association itself, assigned an area of focus and with specific objectives that advance the interests of participants.

Of the responsibilities of staff committee liaison, none is more important than ensuring and promoting the appropriate level of membership participation. If the committee you are staffing was created for vice presidents from member companies, every effort must be made to achieve that level of participation—for example, to avoid a degeneration where assistant vice presidents or lower-level executives serve on the committee. When vice presidents stop coming, serious questions must be asked about the committee's relevance and about how well you are staffing it.

The days of members going to meetings to swap stories with old friends and congenial competitors are gone. Today's corporate executive has one imperative: effectively and productively using his or her time. As a staff committee liaison, you must ensure committee meetings are worth the time members spend attending them. Again, it is a matter of adding value.

In most associations, committees are where the work gets done. If you find yourself averse to this activity, you may want to reconsider a career in association work. Those who enjoy supporting a committee, however, might see it as a training ground for staffing a board of directors, and as an opportunity to grow in their careers.

Teamwork

Working in teams has long been a way of life in associations, reflecting the wide range of functions an association is expected to perform, often with limited staff resources. Certainly for the smaller association, everyone is on the meetings and conventions team, especially in the weeks leading up to the annual meeting and during it. More important than how the teams are organized is the spirit in which they operate. Again, the theme is service—to members and to the goals of the organization. In an association, this means service to others on staff. More precisely, the idea of *association* does not stop at the organization's name; it has to be imbedded in the culture if the association is to thrive.

The people who start and support associations see beyond their own immediate interests toward a larger goal, a broader horizon. They believe in their discipline or industry and are committed to its improvement and growth. A staff that does not share this sense of growth and volunteerism will eventually fail. Never forget that weekend work for staff may be burdensome, but staff receive payment for it. The member sitting next to you is doing the association's work for free. Volunteers' commitment is deep, and they expect no less from those who earn a living from the association. If you do not have a sense that the association's goals and objectives in some way contribute to a better world, you are just putting in the hours.

Associations are created to serve the common goals and interests of their members, not to make their employees rich (although many have enjoyed financial success as association professionals). If you take professional fulfillment from group achievement, association work can be an immensely rewarding. For those suited to it and successful at it, giving is receiving.

CHAPTER 4

Performance Reviews

Just hearing the words "performance review" makes some people shudder. They imagine a stiff, formal meeting in which supervisor and employee sit down once a year to look at a report focused on task completion (below expectations, met expectations, and so forth) next to line items (management, budget, communication, commitment) and discuss the written comments. Then the reviewee signs on the dotted line and gets back to work for another year.

In today's service-driven world, where the most important assets of the organization are likely to be its employees, expectations are no longer based simply on task completion. Instead, a dynamic continuum is at work—a cycle of task completion, task evaluation/enhancement, and staff development, leading to enhanced task completion, further task evaluation and staff development, and so on. In fact, performance evaluations should be viewed much like the strategic plans of associations. They offer you the opportunity to set goals, develop strategies for achieving those goals, establish measurement criteria, and incorporate continual learning into a plan for personal development.

In this world, sitting down once a year for a performance review is not enough. Too many opportunities arise and crises threaten during the year, making it difficult to remember the major achievements and notable missteps 10 or even 12 months ago. Accordingly, many supervisors have come to see performance reviews as something to be done routinely, year-round, and even daily, always encompassing task completion *and* task enhancement and professional development. This does not mean micro-management or nit-picking. It means open and routine communication and the development of

21

a professional relationship where the purpose is not to find fault but to identify opportunity for improvement. Performance reviews should strengthen the staff member's interest in performing by looking at the current ability to perform tasks and how to grow in responsibilities.

It is not the format of the periodic review but the substance of it. Rather than focusing on what was done (task completion) the review focuses on what is expected (task completion, task evaluation and enhancement, and professional development), all in the context of advancing the association's goals. More than measuring the goals achieved or what was done, it concentrates on what is to come. In this way, the formal review becomes something of a strategic plan for the employee.

The practice of year-round performance evaluation reflects the increased value associations place on staff and the greater value staff bring to the job. Your association's particular practices will reflect the management style of the chief executive officer and the association's culture. If you receive continual feedback on how you are performing over the course of a year, be happy and prosper. If not, look for opportunities to foster an atmosphere that is conducive to such an approach. If you continually meet with frustration, if you believe you'll always be evaluated only as a "task completer," think of moving on, because it appears likely that no one is considering moving you up or even furthering your professional development.

In short, performance reviews are how you get better, how you improve. They are not something to be resisted or even feared but rather something to be insisted upon. And you, as an employee, should assume some responsibility for seeing reviews are done right and done well.

Reviewing the CEO

When it comes to the CEO, who is reviewed by the board, year-round performance reviews are simply not practical. Typically, boards meet periodically to evaluate the association's progress against goals already set and to provide direction and new goals for the future. While board members may hope that a CEO continues to develop as a professional, or even expect it, they do not see it as one of their responsibilities. Although responsible for ensuring that those on staff continue to develop professionally, the CEO must take personal responsibility for his or her own professional development. (See Chapter 12.)

Because year-round review is too difficult, the annual review grows in importance. A strategic plan helps by providing a context in which the volunteer leadership provides direction and sets specific goals against which the CEO can manage and lead. A continually changing volunteer leadership presents a communication challenge to the CEO unlike any found in the corporate sector and most other organizational structures. Often, the CEO reports to a continuum of people from a board of directors that, itself, is subject to complete rollover in as few as four years.

Introducing a well-structured, performance-review process can overcome these challenges. Take the example of a CEO's first year in the position. Ideally, after three months on the job, the CEO and board leadership (such as the executive committee) hold an off-site meeting at which the CEO reports on the organization: staff quality, association performance versus the strategic plan, program strengths and weaknesses, state of strategic relationships, advocacy/issue opportunities and threats, and other aspects. The CEO recommends goals for the remaining nine months of the first year's service. Several days before the meeting, the executive committee receives the written report so members can come prepared to discuss the priority goals for the coming nine months. The meeting closes with a discussion and mutual agreement on three to five priority goals to be achieved in the next nine months. The CEO's first-year performance would be measured against these, in addition to standard measures of managerial competence.

In subsequent years, performance reviews would be the same in substance, with adjustments in method. There would be no need for the meeting three months into the year. Also, each association would have to find a balance regarding which volunteer leaders would participate. Certainly, the executive committee would be involved in any evaluation and goal-setting process, but having as many as seven members makes the group too large to meet with the CEO for an annual review.

Some associations convene the executive committee to agree on performance and goal setting for the coming year, leaving it to a "CEO Evaluation Committee" to sit down with the CEO to review the year passed and discuss goals for the coming year. They may ask the immediate past chair, the current chair, and incoming chair to serve on the evaluation committee. This composition facilitates discussion on actions taken by the CEO during the previous year and helps the incoming leadership in focusing on priorities in the years to come. Whatever the evaluation method or process, an annual review of the CEO must be done in some formal and structured manner. That is the way to ensure the goals and interests of volunteer leaders and a CEO do not diverge and separate. A formal and structured review also reaffirms the roles of the volunteer leaders and the CEO.

Doing performance reviews well means creating a culture of trust, open communication, and mutual respect in which employer and employee invest in each other. This commitment to staff and by staff separates dynamic, living organizations from those that only mark time and complete tasks.

A Sample Evaluation

This sample evaluation, developed for CEOs, may look like a report card at first glance. Yet it communicates to the executive committee everything a CEO does. In effect, it sets the agenda for the review and provides a context to discuss the year passed and to discuss what the CEO has accomplished (or didn't).

No one likes hearing they have performed "below expectations," but knowing the views of committee members will alert a CEO to their concerns and provide opportunity to discuss what steps to take to improve performance or strengthen ability in the coming year. Also, the form makes it clear that even an instance of under performance is only one among a full range of responsibilities where performance met or exceeded expectations. It can lessen the effect of a weakness by emphasizing the breadth of a CEO's strengths and accomplishments.

ANNUAL EVALUATION
(Name)

_____

Please indicate your evaluation of the incumbent's performance for the previous 12 months.

	Below Expectations	Met Expectations	Above Expectations	Well Above Expectations
Qualities				
Judgment	____	____	____	____
Leadership	____	____	____	____
Creativity	____	____	____	____
Initiative	____	____	____	____
Flexibility	____	____	____	____
Operating Under Pressure	____	____	____	____
Dependability	____	____	____	____
Skills				
Communication	____	____	____	____
Oral	____	____	____	____
Written	____	____	____	____
Advocacy	____	____	____	____
Policy Development	____	____	____	____

	Below Expectations	Met Expectations	Above Expectations	Well Above Expectations
Consensus Development	____	____	____	____
Decision Making	____	____	____	____
Management	____	____	____	____
Follow-up	____	____	____	____

Duties

BOARD OF DIRECTORS

Communication	____	____	____	____
Meetings	____	____	____	____
Availability	____	____	____	____
Facilitate Policy-making Function	____	____	____	____

STAFF

Leadership	____	____	____	____
Performance	____	____	____	____
Delegation of Authority	____	____	____	____
Hiring, Retention, Development	____	____	____	____
Morale	____	____	____	____
Coordination/Synergy/ Teamwork	____	____	____	____

MEMBERSHIP

Perception of Value by Membership	____	____	____	____
Quality of Membership	____	____	____	____
Quality and Frequency of Participation	____	____	____	____
Growth	____	____	____	____

NONDUES REVENUE PROGRAMS

Revenue Targets	____	____	____	____
Cost Targets	____	____	____	____

	Below Expectations	Met Expectations	Above Expectations	Well Above Expectations
Relevance of Products and Programs to Membership Needs	___	___	___	___
New Product Development	___	___	___	___
NON-REVENUE PROGRAMS				
Government Affairs	___	___	___	___
Regulatory Affairs	___	___	___	___
Communications	___	___	___	___
State and Regional Association Support	___	___	___	___
Spokesperson	___	___	___	___
Relations with Other Associations	___	___	___	___
Coalitions	___	___	___	___
Budget Development and Approval	___	___	___	___
Financial Reporting	___	___	___	___
NOTABLE ACHIEVEMENTS				
In Business and/or Strategic Plan	___	___	___	___
Outside Business and/or Strategic Plan	___	___	___	___

DISAPPOINTMENTS

INCENTIVE KEYS FOR THIS EVALUATION PERIOD

INCENTIVE KEYS FOR NEXT EVALUATION PERIOD

GENERAL COMMENTS

Source: JDG ASSOCIATES, LTD.

CHAPTER 5

Your Resume

The people who read resumes are human. Whether it's the hiring executive or a recruiting professional or researcher going through a stack of resumes, several areas inevitably demand attention: overall presentation and readability, certain key words, the type and culture of employers, and the specific skill areas and experiences of the candidate.

Typically, resumes are separated into three piles: A candidates, B candidates, and "out." After an initial screen of 100 resumes, a second look at the A and B candidates may generate 15 or 20 to review more closely; 10 or 15 of these make the "to call" list. The point is this: Make it easy for the reviewer to see what's important in the first look through the resumes. Buried nuggets generally stay hidden, raising the probability that you will be passed over.

Suggested Format

Following are recommendations from the perspective of an executive recruiter. The elements listed are usually sufficient for the majority of those seeking employment in the association field.

Name and Address should be in bold type and centered at the top of the first page. Include your home, cell, and work phone numbers, plus your e-mail address.

A *Summary* section can be a useful introduction to your employment history section. It should never be more than four or five lines in a two-page resume.

Employment History is the meat of your resume. What the reviewer sees there determines whether your resume moves to the A or B pile. What you are currently doing—or have done most recently—is generally of greatest interest to the reviewer. That's why your employment history should *always* be in reverse-chronology format. Start with your current or most recent job and move backward in your career. Include a clear, brief description of the organization for which you work (or last worked), and what you do (or did) for it. For example:

> Vice President of Operations for the American Widget Association, a Washington, DC-based national trade association with a $5 million annual budget and staff of 25 providing advocacy and member services to 1,400 corporations ranging in size from Fortune 100 to $10 million in annual sales. Report to the President and supervise 14 staff with responsibility for annual meeting/convention; insurance products; and education, training and publication functions, as well as the finance and administration division. 1998 to present.

After establishing the type of organization where you have been successful (the organizational context), specify in bullet form the five or six areas for which you have specific responsibility, followed by four or five specific achievements. After listing your current or most recent position, list the one previous, and then the one previous until you have covered your career. As a general rule, if you have been in the workforce for 10 years or more, you should be able to fill a two-page resume. Three pages is also comfortable, but more than that can get tiresome to the reviewer. Employers don't hire resumes; they read resumes to become acquainted with the parameters of a professional's life at work. If there seems to be grounds for further discussion, the employer will call and perhaps invite you for a screening interview.

As for job history, let's assume you are 40 years old and have had five jobs; the last two go back to when you were 30, and the previous three jobs take you back to your college graduation. On a two-page resume, the two most recent jobs should appear on the first page. For your first three jobs after college, include less information—your title, the type of organization, and brief notes on responsibilities and achievements are sufficient.

The reverse-chronology format contrasts sharply with the functional format, which lists general functions such as management or budget/finance and then describes your achievements in each. If yours is the only resume being reviewed, this might get you noticed. Note, however, that many executive search firms will not even review functional resumes. Reviewers will be drawn more quickly to the resume that enables them to consider a candidate's professional experience in the context of a specific organization and to compare the candidate's skills and achievements to the needs of the position being filled.

Professional Affiliations is where you list membership in organizations such as ASAE or an affiliated society, as well as in discipline-specific groups such as the Public Relations Society of America. While such memberships indicate your dedication to a chosen profession, be careful not to overdo it. Listing five committees in one society or another may leave the impression that you spend more time on your profession than on the job.

Education is where you list the schools you attended, the degrees earned and the years awarded, and the disciplines studied,

Personal is an optional section. Marital status and number of children might be helpful in certain cases, but such information is just as well left off. Community service is usually helpful, but listing a political affiliation, anything of a religious nature, or an affiliation with a specific interest group (for example, the Flat Earth Society) can be hazardous for several reasons. First, the reviewer could have issues with the group. More generally, many reviewers see religious affiliation as a personal matter and are uncomfortable with it in a professional setting. As a general rule, most personal information is best left unmentioned until you are in an interview when you can better gauge its appropriateness.

Note: An *Objective* section is not recommended. It is better to address your objectives in two or three paragraphs in the cover letter, which enables you to tailor your objective to the specific position. If misinterpreted, an objective statement on a resume can move you toward the B or "out" pile before your qualifications are ever considered.

Other tips include:

- Customize your resume. With personal computers readily available, tailor your resume to the specifics of a particular position. For example, if you know the organization well, or even the person who will be reviewing the resume, you might add more personal information that you believe will strengthen your candidacy. You could also emphasize or add certain skills, experiences, or achievements for which the position appears to call. In doing this, never provide misleading information or exaggerate your experience or achievements. The purpose of the resume is to get a call or an opportunity for a face-to-face interview; the last thing you want in an interview is to have to retract or qualify something you claimed in your resume.

- Print your resume on solid color paper, preferably white or eggshell. It should be easily read after copying and faxing. If you have any doubts on this, copy or fax your resume yourself to see how it looks. Some resumes with marbleized backgrounds or colorful borders lose a lot of visual appeal when faxed.

- Use a medium-weight paper. Too heavy a stock can be a nuisance to the reviewer when faxing, copying, or scanning.

- Keep your resume on file in your computer for quick transmittal via the Internet. Be certain of the format it is in and know how to adapt it if necessary to ensure speedy and successful transmission.

Cover Letters

As with format, you'll hear a range of opinions on what constitutes a good cover letter. Because the person who first reads the letter is most likely to be in a screening mode, a two- or three-paragraph letter is generally recommended. Review your letter again and again for grammatical correctness and to ensure no typos appear. In fact, many reviewers view the cover letter as a writing sample: Can this applicant write clearly and form thoughts in concise, easily read paragraphs?

Open the letter by specifying the position for which you are applying, perhaps noting how you became aware of it. Next, introduce your resume. State briefly why you are interested in the position, noting any commonality with the association or its industry or profession. The cover letter is also the place to note any need for confidentiality. Refrain from attempts at humor and familiarity.

In the closing paragraph, thank the reviewer for taking the time to read the resume and to consider your interest and candidacy. Indicate that you will call in a few days to follow up. It can be useful to specify the best time and venue for contacting you.

The whole idea of the cover letter is to transmit and introduce your resume quickly and in a way that promotes a positive expectation in the mind of the reviewer. In other words, it should show you write well; have a clear sense of the position and a reason to be interested in it; and are sufficiently confident to let your experience, skills, and accomplishments speak for themselves.

Sample Resume

Here is an example of a reverse-chronology resume.

Pat Smith, CAE, CMP
1234 Maple Street
Anywhere, USA 09876
H: (123) 456-7890
W: (234) 567-8901
psmith@bpm.com

Employment History

American Widget Association—Year to Present

Vice President of Meetings and Education for this 1,400-member Washington, DC-based national trade association with an annual budget of $5 million and staff of 28. AWA represents its members before Congress and regulatory agencies and provides its members with a full range of services including publications, an annual convention/exhibition, insurance products, and training and education programs. Report to the President and supervise a staff of seven.

RESPONSIBILITIES

Management and sales of annual convention/exhibition.
Supervise education/training division that puts on 70+ seminars and workshops per year.
Supervise off-site publication and video division.
Integration of meetings and education functions with other activities of the Association.
Serve as the acting chief executive officer in the absence of the President.
Management and oversight of AWA strategic-planning process.

ACHIEVEMENTS

Increased annual show and exposition revenue from $1.5 million to $2.6 million.
Negotiated and closed joint publishing agreement for training materials that lowered costs and increased product quality and sales.
Increased member attendance at annual convention by 20% through new member and multiple company representative discounts increasing gross revenue and exposition rentals.
Initiated distance-learning program for seminar and workshop products that also enhanced chapter profile at the local level.

National Association of Widget Distributors—Year to Year

Director of Meetings for this New York City-based trade association representing 2,000 national, regional, and local distributors of widgets and related products. The Association has an annual budget of $3 million and a staff of 17. Reported to the Vice President of Operations.

RESPONSIBILITIES

Registration, promotion, and marketing of annual convention and trade show, including oversight of sales and engagement of commissioned sales agent.

Develop and maintain close working relationship with exhibitors and exhibition management consultant.

Coordination with Education and Training Division of all seminar and workshop programs at the annual convention/exhibition and throughout the year.

Support chapters in their regional meeting programs, including coordination with national seminar and workshop program and national sponsorships for local events.

Management and development of three-person meetings staff.

ACHIEVEMENTS

Increased convention and exhibition attendance by 24 percent in two years.

Increased the percentage of member-company participation in the convention by encouraging the education department to offer a wider range of workshop and training programs.

Facilitated Exhibition Committee meetings, soliciting exhibitor feedback and identifying problems and developing solutions and new service areas.

Society of Widget Designers—Year to Year

Manager of Membership Services of this Chicago, IL-based professional society of 7,000 members in the United States and around the world. With an annual budget of $4 million and a staff of 25, SWD is the internationally recognized leader in the promotion of standards and professional development in widget design, offering continuing education programs and supporting an internationally recognized credential. Reported to the Director of Membership Services.

Responsibilities

Data entry of all membership additions, changes, and deletions necessary to accurately maintain all member records, files, and lists.

Process routine membership inquiries, sending appropriate kits and notifying local associations.

Maintain inventory, assemble and store membership kits and materials.

Handle membership information requests.

Assist and support the Director of Membership Services as requested and needed.

Previous

Worked in retail industry during college and served in administrative staff positions with an insurance agency and a law practice prior to joining the Society of Widget Designers.

Professional Strengths

Strategic planning and organizational visioning
Representation and public speaking
Board liaison and staff management and motivation
Success in and a high degree of comfort with developing nondues revenue income

Education

America State University, 19__, BS in Political Science and General Management

Professional Affiliations and Certification

American Society of Association Executives, Certified Association Executive (CAE)
Meeting Professionals International, Certified Meeting Planner (CMP)
Greater Washington Society of Association Executives

Personal

Like to read, exercise, and participate in community programs.

CHAPTER 6

The Job Search

There are two types of job search: when you have a job and when you don't. Remember: It's much easier to get a job when you already have one. So if you have considered leaving your current position to "really concentrate" on finding a new one, think again. Not liking your current job can be a day at the beach compared to struggling in a job search with declining financial resources, a shrinking list of contacts, and the thrill of seeking a new opportunity fading quickly.

Prospective employers are more favorably disposed toward the candidate with a job, one whose worth is validated by the fact that he or she is being paid to do something right now. Rarely does a prospective employer believe unemployed job seekers came to that situation entirely on their own, that they were not, at the least, nudged out the door. And they question the judgment of a person who would leave one job without having already secured another one. Explaining why you don't have your previous job is not the best way to open an interview for a new position.

With a Job

If you currently have a job, the job search is a part-time job in itself. Like any job, it requires a structured, professional approach. You are probably motivated by career enhancement and professional fulfillment and probably expect a higher salary.

Here are the elements of your job search:

- **Discretion.** Avoid unnecessary risks that would imperil your current position. Exciting though it may be to explore new opportunities, your current employer is likely to have a different view. One exception to this rule in associations is the well-regarded, dedicated professional who is widely viewed as "topped off"—someone whose abilities and performance level are well beyond the needs of the position and who has no place to advance internally. While a job search would not be unexpected in this situation—and may even be encouraged by a chief executive officer committed to professional development—discretion should remain the watchword.

- **Need.** Make sure you have compelling reasons to undertake a job search, and "I'm tired of this place" is not one of them. If you have a job, someone is paying you to do something that the organization needs done. You are of value to the organization, and it pays you in return for your time and energy. Have good reasons to move from that situation, such as increased responsibility or professional enhancement (new skills and experience). You might also be searching for greater compatibility in management styles or a better cultural match. Of course, earning more money is always a consideration in making a move, but it should not be your only reason or even the primary one. Life is too short to spend it doing something you do not find professionally rewarding or stimulating.

- **Outreach.** Once certain you want to leave your current organization, figure out where you want to go. A job search is best done from the perspective of going to a place rather than from leaving one. For starters, look at your Rolodex and e-mail address book. Go through your contacts and organize them into a workable database. Generally, a first cut will break out along the following lines:

  Those a level or two ahead whom you trust enough to discuss making a move. Arrange a breakfast or lunch so you can obtain their counsel, as well as possible sources and leads. After this meeting, they will likely think of you if and when they hear of something appropriate and give you a call. Be alert, however, to hints these people think you are "doing great right now." They may be saying, "You have more growing to do before risking a job search."

  Those currently in a job that appeals to you. Meet them for lunch or coffee and see what their job is really all about and whether they believe you would enjoy and do well at it. These contacts, too, will now be alert to opportunities for you.

  Those who recently landed in a new position. See how they did it—ask about the techniques used, the contacts made, and the risks involved. These people might even know of an open position in which you might be interested.

In addition to mining and developing the contacts you already have, develop entirely new ones. Those in the association profession, especially in major urban areas, have numerous opportunities to attend receptions and other gatherings to meet new people and encounter new organizations. Open your mind to new names and groups, and think tangentially. Where previously you may have sorted those you meet at receptions into those who can help you do your job or not, now add a new category—people who might be useful in your job search.

Be aware, however, that much of what people may say in such circumstances is likely to be inflated. Everyone loves an adventure, and some may succumb to the vicarious pleasure of watching you take a chance they would never dream of. So be careful, realistic, and practical. It's your job and your paycheck that are on the line, not theirs.

- **Competitiveness.** As you initiate a search, qualify the opportunities and prospects that you uncover and encounter. Do you really want the job? In other words, does the position and organization meet your professional and compensation needs? Is it in a cultural setting you would find stimulating? Can you perform in the organization at a level that will meet your standards? And most important: How competitive are you for the position? Being able to do a job is one thing. Being able to do it better than anyone else likely to apply is something else entirely. The decision to pursue a position must include a realistic assessment of how much value you bring compared to others available at the compensation level of the job. You should qualify every opportunity and pursue only those positions you are competitive for in some measurable way—those you have a realistic chance of getting.

- **Thoroughness.** Friends and associates who hear about a good opportunity may not think of you first, especially if you are well placed and successful. So make certain, within your tolerance for risk, that others are aware that you would welcome hearing of new opportunities. Also, never ignore the possibility that the best possible position for you at this time in your career is right where you are. In matters of career development and earning a paycheck, change for change's sake is rarely a good idea.

Without a Job

If you are currently unemployed, a job search is a full-time job. Approach it as such, if possible from a location outside your home that you can go to every day (especially Monday mornings). Your first consideration is probably earning a paycheck, with career development/professional enhancement taking second place.

Leave your home as often as you can, especially after the weekend. Cartoonists and comics might crack wise about the drudgery of returning to work on Monday morning but, for the professional, Monday morning at home means you are out of work and not somewhere where you can add value and grow professionally. Also, being out of work is a particularly good time to evaluate whether you were doing what you want to be doing—and whether you should be doing something else. You might, for example, consider moving from member services to meetings/conventions or to communications.

Following are the keys to a search without a job.

- **Thoroughness.** Once you have decided what type of position to search for, look at newspaper ads, Internet listings, and job banks in professional associations such as ASAE (www.asaenet.org, click on Career Headquarters) and local allied societies or newsletters such as *CEO Job Opportunities Update* (www. associationjobs.com.) There is also the Internet itself, with its job banks, chat rooms, and Listservs. Accessing these online resources is part of a modern-day job search. During the course of your search, make sure you gain access to all available job listings and pursue them as appropriate.

- **Reaching out (not grasping).** As an association professional, you have undoubtedly developed extensive contacts over the years. Go through your Rolodex, e-mail lists, and computer mailing lists. Identify 50 to 100 or so people who would be likely to return your call. Divide the list into groups of 20; in the first week of your search, mail to each a two- or three-paragraph letter explaining your situation and attach a two-page resume. (See Chapter 5.) Personalize the letter as much as possible. In the second week, make follow-up calls to the first 20 people and send another 20 letters. Repeat the process each week.

- **Patience.** Remember when you may have received a letter from an out-of-work colleague. As the person's resume fell onto your desk, you may have thought, "Pat's on the street. Too bad. Dedicated. Works hard. Sure hope that never happens to me. Now, where can I put this thing so I don't have to think about it right now?" Truth is, few who receive such letters quickly reach for the phone. So unless the recipient is a close friend or owes you a big favor, he or she will probably put your letter away. You have to call them.

- **Positive attitude.** When you make the call, anticipate a range of reactions, such as guilt for not calling you when the letter was first received. Put your colleague at ease—thank him or her for taking the call and say you're following up on your letter. Just don't press the issue of whether the person received the letter (you both know he or she did). The advantage is likely to be yours, but only if you are pleasant, enthusiastic, and engaging. Involve the person in a conversation, but make it clear you're seeking help, not a position in his or her organization. If you can accomplish this within the first few minutes, the person will settle down, get comfortable with your situation, and stand ready to help. Try to set up a meeting in your colleague's office, or for breakfast or lunch, so you can demonstrate that you are all right, that this should not have happened to you, and that you would appreciate job-hunting assistance.

At the face-to-face meeting, after the pleasantries, discuss what you see yourself doing in the future and look for the person's reaction. This will help you learn what someone else thinks about you and help you see things about yourself you might not have considered. In addition, it draws someone else into your job search and provides you with more opportunities to network. Also, be certain to ask for the names of additional people this person thinks you should contact in your search.

- **Determination.** Other contact names will crop up throughout the process. Pursue them as appropriate. If you are still looking after two months, send a quick note to those you contacted in the first week to report that your search continues. Provide an update to keep them part of your search. Just make sure the note is upbeat and optimistic. You want everyone on your side, thinking positively of you. Their continued confidence in your ability and attitude is essential.

- **Contact techniques.** Another technique in contact development, useful for those engaged in advocacy, is to approach those whom you were in the business of lobbying and see who else was lobbying them. Say you worked on environmental issues for an association representing a manufacturing

---

The Unemployed Job Seeker

The unemployed job seeker is like the captain of a submarine with a broken periscope who is in the middle of an enemy convoy. When the sonar operator reports ships in every direction, the captain can whine about the broken equipment, say, "It's not my fault," and return to base without engaging the enemy. Or, the captain can fire a torpedo every 15 degrees of the compass and see what happens. On a job search, you want to fire as many torpedoes as you can—and in all directions. To complete your mission, to land a job, you only need *one* hit.

industry. Approach the people you worked with at the Environmental Protection Agency, Congress, or statehouse and ask if they are aware of positions in other industries who are lobbying them. Any meeting that results in a contact name or a new industry is a good meeting.

This can also work for meeting planners. National sales representatives for hotel properties or convention/visitor bureaus are a good source of leads for positions in other associations with heavy convention and meeting agendas. Think of overlapping circles: You are in circle A, which overlaps circle B, which overlaps circle C. A great opportunity for you might exist in circle C, but you won't find out about it unless you develop your contacts in B, which in turn will take you to C. It is the essence of networking—and it's how a lot of jobs, maybe most, are found.

- **Consulting.** Stay active in your field. As you search for a new position, be alert to consulting opportunities. For some disciplines, such as meeting planning and membership development, part-time or consulting opportunities are commonplace. This activity keeps you sharp in your field and provides some income. Most important, it broadens your professional exposure and provides additional contacts for your search. It should also be noted that more than a few successful consulting businesses were built out of part-time work begun as part of a job search.

Bettering the Odds

A job search is an exercise in probabilities. Many job seekers routinely apply for positions well outside their discipline or career track, where their chances of being hired are significantly below those of other applicants. Because association work often requires those in the professional ranks to perform across a wide variety of functions (member services, meetings/conventions, continuing education, communication, and so forth), it is easy to forget that while you can perform in a particular function, you may not be competitive in it.

Adding value to an organization, and quickly, is the driving force behind any hiring decision. The higher the position, the more this principle applies. Devote your time and emotional energy to openings that offer a measurable probability of success.

CHAPTER 7

The Interview

Contrary to popular belief, the primary purpose of an interview is not to get a job. While the ultimate purpose is to receive an offer for the position, the more immediate objective is for the search committee or the hiring executive to get to know you better—and for you to get to know the organization better. Everything you do regarding an interview should address these two objectives. After the hiring executive has gotten to know you, he or she will make the next move—to offer you a position or pass. If the decision is to offer you a position, you can make an informed decision whether to accept the offer or turn it down if you have already done your due diligence.

Never forget what's at the heart of an interview: two parties seeking a mutual solution to each other's needs. The interview is not the beginning of your relationship. It is better seen as a midpoint. The relationship started when you submitted your resume or were otherwise introduced and the organization decided to bring you in for a closer look. When you reach this midpoint, here are some suggestions:

Know the organization. If an employer has committed time to you, make the same commitment. Learn about the organization. The association's Web site is an obvious starting point, but delve deeper. A few minutes on the phone with someone you know who works there or is otherwise familiar with the group can be helpful. During the interview, however, be careful not to give the impression you know all about the organization. Part of the interviewer's job is to provide you with information.

Know the job.   Obtain a position description before you have the interview. An organization chart is also very useful if you can get it without seeming too pushy.

Keep your composure.   Franklin Roosevelt's famous observation, "The only thing we have to fear is fear itself," is appropriately applied to job interviews. It is natural to be nervous for an interview. Just remember, it is a meeting of those with a mutual interest. You are there at the interviewer's invitation. Some interviewers are stern without intending to be; a pleasant, engaging manner on your part will make it easier for both of you.

Engage.   Always concentrate on the fact that an interview is "a getting to know you" exercise. Maintain eye contact, and be certain your body language is natural and appropriate to the discussion. Interviewers may ask many questions, but they are generally interested in having a conversation so they can determine what you know and what sort of person you are. And don't be afraid to ask questions in return. Properly done, this helps promote a dialogue and provides an insight into how you think.

Be prepared to talk about yourself.   Some interviewers will give you a chance to make an opening statement. Take advantage of this because it allows you to lead the discussion. But never take more than five minutes, and don't waste that time simply reciting your resume. Spend a couple of minutes commenting on what you have done, what attracts you to the position, and how you see it fitting with your career goals.

Make the most of the questions.   Don't look at a question as something that demands an answer but rather as an opportunity to present yourself. Think of each question as a discussion point, which means avoiding one-word answers or responses that seem "pat" or packaged. Guard against a "data dump" of facts.

Remember, an interview is more than a test of your specific knowledge. It is an introduction, an opportunity to engage. How you speak—your manner, approach, confidence, and comfort level—is as important as what you actually say. If there is a flat spot in the discussion, fill it with an amplification of what you just spoke about.

Ask your own questions.   Do not leave the burden of the discussion on the interviewer. Be prepared to ask several questions at the end of the interview—but avoid questions about compensation at your first meeting. Pose structural questions: To whom will I report? How does the division in which I would be working interrelate with the other divisions? Ask about the association, the industry in which it operates, and the issues facing it. Such questions not only encourage the sense of mutual interest with the interviewer but also help you decide whether you want to work for the organization.

Practice. If you have not been interviewed recently, have a friend or two conduct mock interviews with you. Get used to hearing a question and turning it into an opportunity to let the interviewer learn about you.

The Little Things

Even seemingly inconsequential actions can influence how an interviewer evaluates you during an interview. Keep these in mind:

ALWAYS BRING A RESUME.

Depending on the type of position you desire, you might also bring writing samples or a portfolio of your work. Do not offer to show your work during the interview unless asked and offer afterward only if it seems appropriate. Having samples to leave behind can be very helpful.

BE ON TIME.

In fact, plan to arrive 15 minutes early—not to the reception area but to the building. Then you'll have extra time built into your schedule in case public transportation is unreliable or you're not able to find a parking place. You can still present yourself to the receptionist five minutes before the interview in a relaxed and composed manner.

WEAR NEUTRAL CLOTHING.

Choose something that you believe is appropriate in a professional environment. Remember, the organization wants to find someone who is comfortable with its culture, not someone interested in making a fashion statement.

AVOID PERFUME AND COLOGNE.

Wearing a scent will not help—and it could hurt your chances.

BE PLEASANT AND ENGAGING.

Good eye contact, a strong handshake, and a confident smile will get an interview off to a strong start. The interviewer is looking for someone to hire; he or she already likes your resume, or you wouldn't be there. In short, the interviewer is predisposed to like you. Reinforce this from the beginning. See yourself as a welcome guest.

PART II

TAKING COMMAND

CHAPTER 8

Making It to Number One

Do you dream of being a chief executive officer, a Number One? Although it's possible to have a fulfilling and successful career without getting to the top spot, the goal remains attractive for many, especially those who have enjoyed success and promotion in their association careers.

Let's take a look at the numbers. In the Washington, DC, area alone, more than 85,000 people work for associations; about 1,100 associations have annual budgets of $1 million or more. If you take out the one-quarter of CEO jobs that usually go to non-association executives, the odds of an association professional making it to the top are approximately one in 100. Rather than be discouraged by these odds, however, you can start charting a course to the top by pondering the following points.

Desirable Qualities

The ultimate arbiter of whether you will land a CEO position is the association's search committee. Members of the search committee are chosen from among volunteer leadership and generally represent different aspects of the membership: East Coast/West Coast, old/young, producers/suppliers, service-oriented/issues-oriented, and so on. The idea is to capture the institutional profile and culture of the association and to include those members who are highly committed to its goals and objectives. They are volunteers, successful in their industry or profession, and distinguished from others by their interest in the world beyond the gates of their factory or the day-to-day concerns of their professional practice. Here's what they look for in candidates (For more information, see Chapter 10).

- **Service-Oriented Attitude.** Search committee members are interested in which direction their industry or profession is headed. They usually see themselves as being in service to the industry or profession and seek CEO candidates who can be similarly committed and are motivated by service to a larger goal. While they welcome creativity, entrepreneurship, and ambition in CEO candidates, committee members look most favorably on someone who will promote the association's goals and well-being.

- **Management Skills.** To win credibility with the staff as a leader and with the board as an executive, management skills are necessary. A CEO who cannot manage will either bring the association to ruin or gradually lose authority to others who can manage. The greatest speech to your association is of little value if there are no chairs in the room for the audience to sit on, or if the microphone was turned off because the bills were not paid, or if the communications department was not given adequate notice to ensure media coverage.

- **Leadership Skills.** An association CEO must also be a leader who brings a sense of purpose to the organization and sets direction. Where the leader motivates others to achieve a shared goal, by example or force of personality, the manager assigns duties and monitors progress in their achievement. Where the leader assumes authority to achieve a goal, a manager is given authority and accepts instruction in its application and use. Managers keep an organization functioning; leaders focus on why the organization exists and where it is going.

    A leader is comfortable with change and understands that change is inevitable. Search committees respond to people who see a CEO position as an opportunity for accomplishment, to do something with the organization in the interest of its members. Leadership is not for everyone. It is far more than a nice way to close a career. It must be something you have been doing and building on all along.

A Good Fit

Attitude, management, leadership—these qualities will make you a serious contender. But there is still the question of "fit." Does the search committee like you? Do you appear to be someone with whom they want to spend time away from their work and family while attending to the association's business? You are asking them to trust you with the welfare and future of their association, so it should not be surprising they want to like the person they select as CEO.

On your part, with what type of organization and membership are you most effective and comfortable? The more successful you are in one type of association may mean you are less likely to be successful in another type. For example, success with an issues-driven trade association, whose board looks to the CEO to drive the agenda and serve as spokesperson, does not automatically translate into success as the CEO of a professional association with a highly participative board that believes only a member should serve as the association's spokesperson. Each group requires an executive with a different professional makeup.

Numerous executives have taken a position for the honor and prestige of serving as a CEO, rather than because it fit their skill set and personality. Of course, taking the wrong job as an association CEO will not be for eternity; it will only seem that way. The ordeal is generally over in a year or so, with the CEO leaving among angst and regret and with finger-pointing on all sides.

Thousands of professionals have had rewarding and fulfilling careers in association management without ever having been a CEO. If you truly want to serve as a Number One, keep in mind that it is a career goal built on competence in management, achievement in leadership, and the ability to take satisfaction from group success and service to others.

Being Second in Command

Serving as a Number Two—a deputy chief staff executive—is often seen as a natural step toward the top spot of CEO. Successful managers outside the profession—from academia, private industry, or the government—see it as a good place to enter the association profession. They believe the Number Two slot will allow them to use their basic management skills while they learn the association environment.

These expectations seem plausible, yet they are often unrealistic. In fact, relatively few associations are large enough to warrant a designated Number Two. As a general rule, a full-time deputy executive is not needed until the association's staff numbers 40 or more. In many associations, the number-two position is a de facto assignment awarded to the CEO's direct report whose responsibilities represent the most important service the association provides to its members. Other associations shy away from a second-in-command of any nature. The reasons for this range from the inspired (naming a deputy would lessen the synergistic relationship of a smoothly functioning senior executive staff) to the mildly paranoid (naming a Number Two will threaten the CEO's position with the board).

In rare circumstances, a Number Two position is created as part of an orderly succession plan. The Number Two joins the staff a year or so before the incumbent CEO's departure, ensuring time for the ropes to be learned and the contacts passed on. More commonly, the board takes the occasion of the incumbent's departure to review and possibly reorient the association's direction.

Association boards often view the executive suite as having two elements: leadership and management. This can play out in several ways, such as the outside/inside scenario. In this, the CEO serves as the spokesperson and visionary while the Number Two manages the day-to-day operations. This often happens in professional associations where the CEO is a peer (for example, a doctor or lawyer) who represents the association to those whose groups it wishes to reach. The Number Two is then an association professional whose primary responsibilities range from running the government relations/policy apparatus to overseeing the annual meeting/tradeshow to paying the bills.

When looking at a Number Two position to enhance your career, research the type of association you are considering. A non-peer Number Two in a professional association may be excluded by tradition, or even the by-laws, from ever assuming the CEO slot. A similar obstacle may exist in a trade association with an established practice of looking to the industry for CEO candidates. Whether an association is issues- or services-driven is also critical. In the former, a Number Two position whose responsibilities are largely managerial is unlikely to be tapped to succeed as CEO. In a services-driven association, however, the Number Two with strong managerial skills could expect to have a leg up on the competition.

Also look at how much the Number Two position links your career to that of the CEO. It is not uncommon in an involuntary separation for the Number Two to be asked to leave along with the CEO. Evaluate this risk in view of the strength of the CEO with the board and your working relationship with the CEO. Will you be close enough to the CEO to help him or her maintain a strong and positive relationship with the board and membership?

The road to becoming an association CEO is not always smooth, and serving as Number Two is no guarantee of achieving that goal. More important than being Number Two is understanding the leadership function of the CEO and developing your own leadership skills and qualities accordingly. In other words, no matter what your current position, be a CEO in approach and outlook.

Reaching Consensus

Associations, by their very nature, are consensus animals. They are formed by people or corporations having similar interests who join together to achieve common objectives. Once this consensus is broken, no matter the cause, the association will decline in influence and effectiveness until consensus is restored.

Differences on a major issue facing the industry or profession—dues structures, program development, and the style and perceived effectiveness of staff management —can all lead to a loss of consensus. For professionals whose livelihood depends on a consensus of the whole, a split within the group has a telling effect on morale, productivity, and, eventually, staff retention. The long-term effect of any division is generally less apparent to those on whom it may well have the greatest effect: the membership.

A lack of consensus can be especially devastating to an issues-driven association, which represents its members before legislative and regulatory bodies at the federal and state levels. If the association can no longer claim to represent the majority of the industry or profession, access to decision makers suffers. An association's influence and credibility are based on years of "being there." As it loses its place and role, turning the situation around becomes more difficult with each passing day.

In an association with full-time staff, the CEO has much of the responsibility for reaching and maintaining consensus. He or she must understand and anticipate the needs of the membership over time and assist the volunteer leaders in pointing the group in the direction indicated. Although the membership retains ultimate responsibility for consensus, the CEO plays a key role.

Corporate CEO Versus Association CEO

How does the CEO of an association differ from the CEO of a corporation? Certainly, you'll find many similarities in the responsibilities of the two positions, including budget, management, and strategic planning. The differences lie in how associations are structured.

Traditionally, hierarchical organizations are depicted graphically as a triangle. (See Figure 3.) In the corporate model, the CEO sits at the pinnacle as a full member of the board, with direct reports at the next level and the remainder of staff in various layers beneath. They all work to achieve the goals and objectives, which are seen primarily as those of the CEO, under the ultimate direction of the board of directors.

Whereas a corporation has one hierarchy, an association has two: the membership and the staff. In an association, the membership is usually

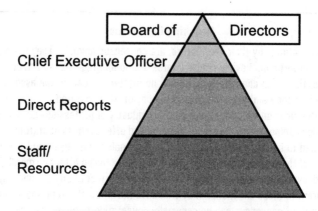

FIGURE 3. THE CORPORATE MODEL

structured in a traditional hierarchical manner: a chief elected officer, usu-ally the chair, a board of directors, and the general membership, with allow-ance for committees and task forces as needed. The staff is also structured hierarchically—the CEO at the top, the direct reports (vice presidents and directors) next, and the balance of the staff beneath.

In the association model, these organizational triangles are joined at their respective pinnacles, with the staff triangle at the bottom and the membership triangle on the top and inverted. (See Figure 4.) Understand-ing the relationship between the two organizational triangles, one repre-senting the membership and the other representing staff, illuminates the qualities and skills a CEO needs.

The membership founded the association—the members are the rea-son it exists. They are the ultimate judge of its utility and success. The staff—employing resources such as publications, meetings/trade shows, and the association's reputation—are committed to achieving the goals and ob-jectives. Linking the membership and the staff is the CEO. He or she con-nects what the membership wants with the resources needed to get the job done. Strong management skills—overseeing finances, operations, and em-ployees—are essential, as would be the case in any enterprise. In managing an association, however, the CEO does not report to a board of directors of a publicly held corporation but to a group of leaders who see their profes-sional, commercial, or personal interests as being directly affected by the management and success of the organization.

The CEO facilitates the membership's efforts to identify its goals and objectives and assists volunteer leaders in coming to a consensus on policies and programs to achieve these objectives. The chief elected officer position

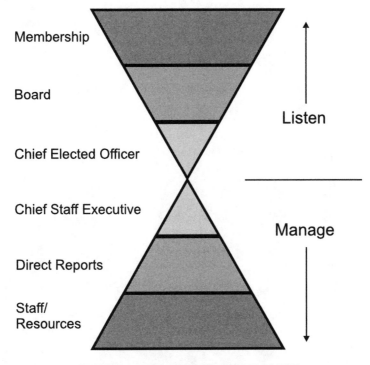

Membership

Board

Listen

Chief Elected Officer

Chief Staff Executive

Manage

Direct Reports

Staff/
Resources

FIGURE 4. THE ASSOCIATION MODEL

also has a responsibility for consensus development. But if the person elected to fill this position does not bring this quality and skill to his or her term in office, the CEO must be prepared to facilitate a continuing consensus. The CEO is also responsible for program implementation. The CEO must, then, be both facilitator and manager. In effect, the CEO listens up and manages down.

To succeed at this balancing act, especially because the chief elected official generally changes every year, flexibility is essential. So while strong leadership qualities are desired, the CEO must have an ego that can find fulfillment and satisfaction in the organization's success rather than in personal recognition. And this flexibility cannot be a fleeting phenomenon; it must remain over time.

CHAPTER 9

Executive Recruiters

Since the early 1990s, association search committees have been increasingly inclined to use executive search consultants in filling chief executive officer (CEO) vacancies. This is particularly true for trade associations and professional societies with annual budgets of $5 million or more. And while the benefits to using a professional recruiter maybe seen as largely falling to the search committee, there are advantages to potential candidates as well.

First, without a recruiter, potential candidates who are not currently seeking a position would never be considered by the committee. As their name implies, executive search consultants *search*. They make the calls, develop the contact sheets, use databases, and draw on candidates met in earlier searches, all to find executives with backgrounds and achievements that match the position's profile. Strong candidates for a position—including those who may not have even been looking—are thus brought into a search they might have otherwise not known about.

Second, the recruiter has the time to meet the candidates when they are available, not when search committee members can break away from their full-time work. And, having learned the culture of the association and knowing what the committee is looking for, the recruiter can limit serious discussions to candidates who meet the basic needs of the position and have a measurable prospect of winning the job. Some candidates complain about not meeting with a committee they "just know" would like them. In the vast majority of cases, however, if you are not selected in the early stages of a search, the recruiter has saved you not only time but also a futile emotional investment in an opportunity you had little chance of winning.

When a search committee uses a recruiter, candidates are interviewed in advance and the committee receives a report with all the relevant information. That means the interview with the association will focus on who you are, rather than an exchange of facts to see what you know. The job interview itself will be structured so that each candidate is reviewed on similar criteria and thus objectively reviewed and evaluated. Also, the recruiter will be certain that you are aware of and comfortable with the salary range and benefits of the position. Committees rely on recruiters to bring them only candidates who will be available at a compensation level they can afford, which is to everyone's advantage.

What to Expect

The professional executive recruiter approaches a search from the perspective of having one client and two responsibilities. The recruiter's first responsibility, of course, is to the client, to present the association with the best candidates in the time allowed for the search and considering the needs of the position (skill profile, experience, compensation range, and so forth). For the candidates, the recruiter also has responsibilities.

Here is what you should expect a recruiter to do.

- Hold your interest in the position in confidence.
- Explain clearly why the position is available, what the job entails, and what is needed to succeed in the position.
- Convey the culture of the association. For instance, is it driven by services or issues? Is it member- or staff-driven? What is the board accustomed to regarding the CEO leadership role? What type of CEO leadership role has been the norm? Are the member companies family owned, large businesses, or a combination?
- Describe the financial condition of the organization, as well as any outstanding legal issues that the association is engaged in that are likely to affect the first year of the new CEO's tenure.
- Communicate salary and benefit parameters, as well as whether a contract will be offered and what it would cover.
- Review the particulars of the association, such as staff tenure, the state of relations between staff and the volunteer leaders, strategic relations with competing and companion organizations, recent program performance, and any changes in direction or emphasis planned by the leadership.
- Ensure you have background information to prepare for the interview. This includes the association's audited financials, bylaws, strategic plan, budget

for current year, and publications. Such information not only enables you to demonstrate your ability to serve in the position, but also prepares you to interview the committee and determine whether the position is a good fit. Note, however, that the recruiter is only a conduit; responsibility for verifying information about the association rests with you as the candidate.

- Support you throughout the search process by returning phone calls, arranging interviews, and so forth. For the final candidates, the recruiter acts as a manager or handler and should be viewed as such.

Executive Recruiters at Work

Here are the tasks an association hires an executive search consultant to perform. Reviewing these will give you a good sense of how a search unfolds and of what you, as a candidate, can expect at each stage.

Preparation

- Assist in defining the position and developing a CEO profile for committee approval.
- Specify position requirements (degrees, years of experience, and so forth).
- Identify the attractiveness of the position to potential candidates.
- Assist in focusing on the association's competitiveness in salary, benefits, and other areas.
- Provide a sense of the market for the position in question.
- Focus on the resource relationship between the position and other members of the staff.
- Prepare a position announcement that will ensure that those who see it will easily understand the position and its potential.
- Develop a search plan (who should be contacted and who should not).

Search

- Identify existing resources in the field.
- Identify association resources, such as contacts of membership and existing staff.
- Prepare mailings and initiate appropriate follow-up.
- Determine freedom to contact companion or competitive associations.
- Identify candidates from previous searches to be resources or candidates.
- Make calls and follow the leads.
- Meet with candidates on their schedules.

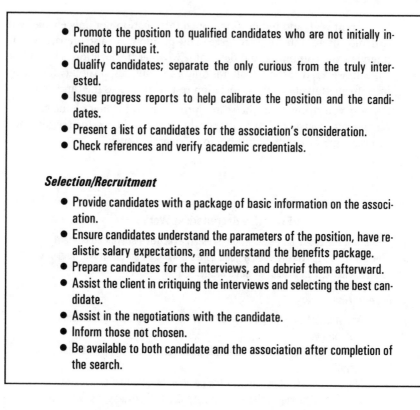

- Promote the position to qualified candidates who are not initially inclined to pursue it.
- Qualify candidates; separate the only curious from the truly interested.
- Issue progress reports to help calibrate the position and the candidates.
- Present a list of candidates for the association's consideration.
- Check references and verify academic credentials.

Selection/Recruitment

- Provide candidates with a package of basic information on the association.
- Ensure candidates understand the parameters of the position, have realistic salary expectations, and understand the benefits package.
- Prepare candidates for the interviews, and debrief them afterward.
- Assist the client in critiquing the interviews and selecting the best candidate.
- Assist in the negotiations with the candidate.
- Inform those not chosen.
- Be available to both candidate and the association after completion of the search.

Internal Candidates

Recruiters are at risk to at least one bias: It is against the internal candidate—someone already on staff who is seeking the CEO position. Not surprisingly, recruiters like to show what they can do, and there is a certain pride in concluding a search with a candidate whom the committee would not have been able to find on its own. This bias can be aggravated by resentment on the part of the internal candidate who often sees the recruiter as an outsider and an obstacle to winning the job. These biases can deny the search committee a good look at a person who may be the best candidate.

The experienced recruiter should be aware of the bias and be able to neutralize it. If you are an internal candidate for a position, guard against any feelings of resentment. Relax and take a step back. Examine the position and what you bring to it, then develop a clear view on what is needed to succeed in the CEO position. Based on your attitude, management skills, and leadership ability, objectively evaluate how strong of a candidate you really are.

Because the recruiter must work between the internal candidate and the search committee, communication between the recruiter and the candidate is generally guarded. However, this should not prevent you from developing a relationship with the recruiter so that the "real you" becomes apparent. A positive relationship with the recruiter—who has prepared the position profile and whose first interest is in finding and presenting the best possible candidates—can be invaluable. If he or she believes you are a legitimate candidate, you will be presented.

CHAPTER 10

What Search Committees Look For in a Chief Executive Officer

When a search for a chief executive officer (CEO) begins, a search committee may have only a notional idea of what it wants. A common point of departure is the most recent executive, as in "We need someone exactly like Pat," or "exactly the opposite of Pat," or "like Pat on leadership, but a better manager." The committee's first task should be to develop a profile of the executive needed. This exercise gives committee members a sense of what their differences and priorities are and lays the groundwork for compromise and consensus as the search progresses.

What do search committees look for in a CEO? There is no stock answer, no magic formula. Each association requires its CEO to have a unique set of skills and qualities, and the committee should identify these before the search begins, preferably in a profile. Fit is what can make an executive a strong candidate for one position and exclude the same candidate from another position, despite the fact that the two associations may seem quite similar.

The CEO Profile

Although the results vary from one association to the next, the process of developing a CEO profile typically requires a search committee to answer these questions:

1. Where do leaders of the association want it to be in three years? This would be discussed by the consultant during in-depth interviews with each member of the search committee and other volunteer leaders as appropriate.

2. What type of person is needed to take the association to that point? The discussion here often centers on the differences between an association CEO and the CEO of a corporation or university or other organization. (See Chapter 8.) The corporate CEO normally assumes a leadership role within the board, playing a dominant role in direction setting, while managing the resources beneath. The association CEO helps the chair, the board of directors, and members determine where they want the organization to go and what they want it to do, then manages the resources to achieve this. In effect, a CEO listens up and manages down.

3. Is the association issues-driven or service-driven? Few associations are exclusively one or the other; most require capabilities in both areas, with a greater emphasis on one. An issues-driven association will require candidates with strong political skills, professionals who can understand members' needs and the outside forces affecting the association, then make good judgments as to what is possible and how best to achieve it. Instincts in consensus development are particularly important, in addition to strong management skills. Service-driven associations generally look for candidates with strengths in management and marketing, with experience in product and service development and revenue generation also prized. Accordingly, CEOs of service-driven associations are more likely to see their association from a business-model perspective.

4. Is the association member- or staff-driven? In other words, is the association in greatest need of a leader or a manager? Associations that see themselves as staff-driven are inclined to search for candidates with strong leadership capabilities; those that describe themselves as member-driven are more attracted to candidates with strengths in management. The successful CEO must have basic skills in each area. Also, after the hire, the sooner the successful candidate demonstrates an ability to manage the association's affairs, the sooner the volunteer leaders will be inclined to look to the CEO to play a leadership role.

5. What are the top three reasons members join and stay with the association? A consultant might query the committee on the most important benefits now, what they were three or four years ago, and what they might

Signs of Change

What is needed to succeed as a CEO changed dramatically during the 1990s, thanks to changes in associations themselves. Dues now constitute less than half of most associations' revenues, reflecting members' insistence on identifying value received for money paid. "Cherry picking," where members pay for the specific services or products they need or use, has grown in popularity. Rather than resist this change, successful CEOs welcome it as an opportunity to show their association remains relevant to the professional objectives of its individual members or the business needs of its corporate members.

There has also been a decline in the one-week annual meeting, which doubled as a vacation for members. Two-career families and increased responsibilities have prompted many associations to offer instead two-day business events, with sporting and entertainment opportunities available before or after for those who have the time. The culture of many associations has changed and intensified such that members want identifiable value for the time and resources they are asked to provide. To be seen as a viable CEO candidate, you must show strong prospects of delivering on this value proposition.

As CEOs have succeeded in this value-added environment, they have come increasingly to see themselves as partners with the volunteer leaders and the board. While search committee members, especially those in trade associations, generally welcome candidates who speak in terms of a partnership with the board, they rarely use this term themselves. "Partnership" implies equality, and search committees rarely lose sight of the fact that they are searching for someone to work *for them.* While the board and the CEO will have a wide range of mutual interests, they are not equals. Volunteer leaders, however, do welcome a CEO who approaches the relationship in the spirit of partnership—in other words, one built on trust and mutual respect. The executive who undertakes the responsibilities of a CEO in this spirit of partnership is likely to be treated as one.

be three or four years in the future. This discussion helps focus the committee's thoughts on the type of candidates they want to see.

6. Is the CEO expected to serve as the principal spokesperson for the association? If so, then communication and presentations skills and experience are important.

7. How important is knowledge of the industry or profession?

8. Are there any financial or legal issues that might adversely affect the attractiveness of the position to potential candidates?

9. How do committee members regard the quality and skill level of the current staff? The answers to this may directly affect the skill set the new CEO

must arrive with to serve effectively—or the people the CEO must hire soon after coming on board.

10. What two or three things must the new CEO achieve in the first 12 months to earn a B+ or better rating?

In addition, an executive search consultant reviews the association's publications, budget reports, financial statements, recent board meeting minutes, and strategic plan and conducts on-site interviews of the association's senior staff.

Peer Leadership

Peer leadership refers to the situation where the CEO is chosen from the membership of the association. (For example, the CEO of the American Widget Association came from the ACME Widget Company.) While associations generally look to association professionals to serve in the CEO role, some favor candidates from their membership ranks. If you are interviewing for a position as a CEO, determine whether association professionals will be considered seriously and given a genuine chance of being selected.

Evaluating an association in the following areas might help you figure that out.

ISSUES- VERSUS SERVICE-DRIVEN

Search committees from issues-driven associations tend to give more consideration to the benefits of peer leadership. Because credibility is crucial to representing the association effectively, they believe the best person to speak for an industry or profession is someone from it. On the other hand, an association professional experienced in issues management will better understand the workings of government and the interplay of organizations that affect policy development and how to position the association to promote its members' interests.

Search committees of service-driven organizations often focus on management skills. Members of such organizations generally look to their association to provide training, credentialing, insurance, and other services. Skills in providing these services can be developed in one association and easily transferred to another. Success in the industry or profession may not necessarily translate to success in association management.

QUALITY AND SIZE OF STAFF

A weak or inexperienced staff would generally indicate the need for a CEO with proven management experience. Association management skills are generally transferable, so a strong, experienced executive can have a dramatic and immediate influence on a staff operating at suboptimum levels. For a group with a larger staff that is well-regarded by the membership, peer leadership may be attractive. This is especially true if the association has a designated Number Two position that is or can be filled by an association professional.

FINANCIAL CONDITION

A financially strong organization with popular programs and services may not require the association management experience that a troubled one might. For the troubled association, however, the skills that the experienced association professional would bring (marketing, membership development, nondues income programs, and so forth) can mean the difference between success and failure.

HOMOGENEITY OF MEMBERSHIP

Association members may have significantly different views on an issue. If this situation exists, hiring a peer as the new CEO may be seen as favoring one faction of the membership over others. Trade associations often represent several different segments of an industry (for example, manufacturers and distributors) and drawing on one or the other of these can also prove fractious. The ability to reach consensus on issues and programs, to promote the common interests of the entire membership, is essential in any association. Any candidate whose background is more likely to threaten consensus than promote it would be viewed less favorably.

DEMOTION

On being hired, the peer technically undergoes a demotion. The reason is that a CEO is in service to the membership—the peer CEO becomes the employee of those in the peer group. The actual status of the peer CEO, of course, will depend on the association's culture and the CEO's management and leadership role. Most peers have no difficulty with this transition. Others do, however, and it can lead to disappointment for both the new CEO and the membership.

A Strategic Decision

From the search committee's perspective, the profile is likely to change during the course of the search process, reflecting the fine tuning that goes on in the minds of committee members and the fact that the candidates they review will have an influence on the type of person they want. In fact, if properly prepared and interviewed, the candidates will help the committee clarify its views on what is needed in the CEO.

On meeting you as a candidate, committee members will usually have one of three basic reactions: "That's just what we're looking for," "That's not what we're looking for," and "That's not what we were looking for, but

---

Role of the CEO

A definition of the CEO's role, which has resonated well with search committees, came from an interview conducted with senior staff during a CEO search. In this interview, the departing executive had been in the position more than 10 years and was well regarded by the staff. The senior members were asked, "What do you need from the CEO to do your job?" The question stumped the first three staff members. The fourth, however, answered, "What we need from the CEO is to ensure that this association remains relevant to the needs of our members." This could be the best one-sentence description of what an association CEO does.

---

it may be what we need." You cannot change what you have to offer the association—that has taken 20 or more years of professional and personal development. But, because of your strengths in skill areas, experience, attitude, and career profile, you may change how the committee defines the needs of the position. This happens frequently. In deciding on the final candidate, the committee is making or confirming a decision on the strategic direction of the association.

As a candidate, being aware of the strategic nature of the hiring decision is critical. A search committee that has not taken the time to determine what it really needs nor understands that choosing a CEO is perhaps the most strategic decision an association's leaders can make, is highly unlikely to know what it is looking for or wants. Never forget that you are interviewing the association as well as being interviewed. Make certain the search committee members know what they are looking for and can say clearly what you must do to succeed as the CEO. Wowing a search committee that doesn't know what it wants—or can't tell you what the association needs—could lead to frustration or ruin once you're on the job.

CHAPTER 11

The Employment Contract

Employment contracts are now commonplace for the newly hired chief executive officer (CEO) of a national professional or trade association. For years, association boards had resisted the use of contracts because they routinely protected the CEO's income for the entirety of the contract term (often three years and as much as five). A board unhappy with an executive's performance in the early years of a contract had to either buy out the balance of its obligation, which might have severely strained the financial resources of the association, or keep an underperforming CEO and hope for the best.

Severance-pay clauses, however, have grown in popularity. These allow the board to terminate an executive without cause before the full term of the contract, say on 6 or 12 months' notice. The greater use of contracts may also reflect the increasing professionalism and quality of those serving as association CEOs. Through the 1960s and 1970s, association boards commonly chose CEOs from among their membership ranks, and contracts among people who knew one another may have been unseemly. As association boards increasingly hired executives with demonstrated skills and experience in association management and issues advocacy, they encountered candidates who, secure and content in their current positions, were not inclined to accept an offer without a contract that contained a measure of income protection.

Another contributing factor: the increased use of performance incentives in CEO compensation packages. As boards focus more on performance and goal achievement, they are increasingly inclined toward incentives. An employment contract is a convenient venue to do this.

Points to Cover

While CEO contracts can run more than 15 pages and cover a wide range of specifics, several core issues should be covered:

Compensation and Benefits. As a candidate for a CEO position, find out early what sort of compensation package is possible. Salary is the simple part of the equation; healthcare and retirement benefits are more complicated to evaluate. For instance, the difference between employee-only and full-family health coverage can be as much as $1,000 a month in after-tax income. Retirement packages also differ widely and across a range of considerations: amount committed, the strength and nature of the commitment, vesting periods, how much must be deferred, and so forth.

You may face the dilemma of trading benefits to get a better job. If you have a particularly strong benefits package at your current employer, you may have to give it up to accept an opportunity at another organization with a weaker benefits package but one that would give your career a significant boost or even redefine it. While healthcare and retirement benefits are important, fixing too closely on benefits can blind you to opportunities that would significantly expand your professional horizon.

Incentive provisions are now commonplace in CEO contracts. CEOs increasingly see themselves as directly responsible for the financial performance of the association, as well as its ability to affect public policy decisions, and they want their compensation to reflect their success. A bonus check of 10 to 15 percent can certainly confirm that it has been a good year.

Boards have been slow to see the benefits of incentives, perhaps because they see such provisions as a compensation issue rather than a management tool. Properly implemented, incentive provisions significantly enhance communication between the CEO and the board by identifying the top three to five areas of concern against which a bonus will be earned. During the course of the year, the CEO will ensure that the chief elected officer is aware of progress in each of these areas; if progress becomes impossible for reasons beyond the control of the CEO, the CEO should alert the chief elected officer and seek agreement on another goal to achieve. Some boards, most notably those of trade associations, now look at part of the CEO's compensation as being "at risk." The thinking is that such an approach promotes a performance and value-added culture within the association's staff, making it more like the private sector.

Annual Evaluation. The provision outlining the method and timing of the CEO's annual review should specify which volunteer leaders will participate and the dates by which it must be completed each year. The evaluation should cover the full the range of the CEO's responsibilities and achievements over the review period measured against objectives and goals agreed upon in advance.

At the time of the annual review, the CEO and the reviewing body should agree on the major goals for the next review period, whether or not the contract contains an incentive provision. With boards constantly changing, an annual evaluation is an excellent mechanism for the CEO and volunteer leaders to focus on what needs to be accomplished over the course of the next review period. (See Chapter 4.)

Specification of Duties. The contract or an attachment should specify the CEO's duties, responsibilities, and authorities and a clear statement as to whom the CEO reports. This is commonly in the form of a board-approved position description, or it may be included in the association's bylaws.

At a minimum, the contract should include a statement specifying the CEO's authority regarding the hiring and firing of staff, staff compensation, and staff size and structure. This is not to recommend complete autonomy for the CEO in all these areas but rather to make clear the necessity, from the outset, of discussing how much autonomy the board allows the CEO.

Terms and Conditions of Cancellation. This provision covers the ways the contract can be canceled, either by the association or the CEO. Some clauses are routine, such as those covering the death or disability of the CEO or malfeasance on the part of CEO (cancellation for cause). Still, have these reviewed by a lawyer.

Cancellation without cause—in other words, "This isn't working out and we want to get someone else in here"—is the severance clause. Understand its provisions and the protection it offers. The length of severance should be based on how long it would take you to find another CEO position, with the expectation that those who relocated will have more difficulty than those in a metropolitan area who have long-established professional contacts. As a general rule, if you are joining an association in the same metropolitan area, six months' severance is a reasonable request. For a position that would move you from, say, Chicago to Washington, it would not be unreasonable to request 12 months.

This section of the contract usually addresses the notice period you must give if departing voluntarily. Do not exceed 90 days' notice. A period longer than this will severely limit your ability to take another opportunity. And, in most cases, an association can identify and sign a new CEO in 90 days. Search firms routinely go from initiation of a search to presentation of final candidates in 8 to 10 weeks.

Relocation. Have a good idea of what the association is willing to consider before you go to the final interview. Associations routinely cover relocation expenses for new hires, especially for a new CEO. Those from corporate backgrounds, however, may be disappointed in the expenses covered and the amounts allowed. Typically, relocation expenses include an allowance for temporary housing and several trips for the family to find a place to live. Real-estate commissions on the sale of a property are rarely covered, although assistance with the closing costs on a new property can usually be negotiated. What is commonly agreed to is an allowance with a cap that will cover specific types of expenses. Also, consult with your accountant on the tax consequences of relocation expenses.

Other areas covered in a typical contract include starting date, conflict of interest, intellectual property, indemnification, arbitration of disputes, and governing law.

Take a Good Look

Because the association is often eager to finalize a hire as soon as possible after selecting the best candidate, it helps to review a draft contract before the final interview. Serious obstacles can then be identified and addressed beforehand. The draft contract would leave blank the compensation, starting date, and other particulars to be agreed upon with the final candidate. In general, honesty, openness, and common sense on everyone's part leads to a successful negotiation. Do not, however, sign anything without your lawyer's advise. Asking for two or three days to review a contract with legal counsel is common, even expected.

A Sample Contract

This model contract was developed for the American Society of Association Executives (ASAE) by Jerald Jacobs, a partner in the Washington, DC, law firm of Shaw Pittman. Numerous search committees have used it in negotiations with candidates.

In addition to covering the basics, the ASAE contract includes certain benefits, (for example, an automobile or a club membership) that do not constitute a measurable tax advantage to the executive. Given that a car can be viewed as lavish by volunteer leaders—especially those from small or family-owned businesses—insisting on it without demonstrating a clear and direct benefit to the association can adversely affect an

---

otherwise positive contract negotiation. Remember to keep your eye on the prize, not on the trappings.

Note: A contract does not have to be in this form to bind both parties. A letter of agreement or a written understanding specifying the terms, conditions, obligations of service, and consideration, signed by both parties, constitutes a contract enforceable under law.

Employment Agreement

This Agreement is made between the _____, a _____ nonprofit corporation (the "Association"), and _____ (the "Executive"), for mutual consideration, the receipt and adequacy of which are acknowledged by the parties, who agree:

1. *Term, Nature, and Review.* The Executive is engaged to serve as _____ of the Association for a _____-year period from _____ to _____. This Agreement will automatically renew each year on _____ for additional one-year periods unless the Agreement is cancelled by the Association or the Executive according to the provisions of Paragraph 4; the Agreement may not be terminated by non-renewal but only by cancellation. The Executive will exert the Executive's full time and energy to the Executive's duties as _____ of the Association. Those duties are specified by the Association's bylaws and other governing documents. They may be supplemented from time to time by the Association's Board of Directors or by the Association's Executive Committee as delegated by the Board. The Executive reports to the Board of Directors or to the Executive Committee when either is in session; otherwise the Executive reports to the elected President of the Association. The Executive is the chief employed officer of the Association with full authority for the management of its affairs subject only to the duties specified by the bylaws or other governing documents or to the direction of the Board, the Executive Committee, or the President. The Executive has sole and exclusive authority for the engagement and discharge of all other employees of the Association. The performance of the Executive will be reviewed annually by the Association's Executive Committee prior to the anniversary date of this Agreement based upon performance criteria and goals provided in writing to the Executive at the beginning of the period under review. The Executive will be employed at the headquarters office of the Association in the _____ area.

2. *Compensation.* The salary of the Executive is _____ per year during the first year of this Agreement, from _____ to _____, payable according to the Association's regular salary payment schedule. The salary of the Executive for subsequent years of this Agreement will be negotiated and agreed by the Executive and the Association's Executive Committee following the annual performance review. In no event, however, will the Executive's salary for any subsequent year of this Agreement be reduced below the level of the previous year. The Executive is entitled to those employee benefits described in the Board-approved Association em-

ployee benefit schedule for the Association's _____ , including participation in the Association's qualified pension plan, family coverage hospitalization and major medical insurance, and _____ business days vacation each year (subject to limitations on carry-forward of accrued, unused vacation days as follows: _____). This compensation constitutes the entire payment by the Association for the services of the Executive. No other or additional compensation in any form will be considered or paid for the period of this Agreement.

  3. *Business Expenses*. The Association will pay, or reimburse the Executive, for reasonable business expenses incurred by the Executive which are directly related to the performance of the Executive's duties of employment, subject to maintenance of documentation by the Executive and review by the Executive Committee. In particular, the Association will pay for the Executive's expenses of membership, receipt of publications, and participation in the activities of the American Society of Association Executives, the _____ Society of Association Executives, and the _____ . The Association will maintain a membership for the business meal and entertainment use of the Association at a private lunch, country or yacht club, with any personal use by the Executive reimbursed to the Association. The Association requires that the Executive's spouse attend and participate at those Association or association-community events or meetings which the Executive's spouse can conveniently attend, subject to approval annually by the Executive Committee of the Association; and the Association will reimburse the Executive fully for this spouse travel and other related expenses, as well as for the personal federal income tax, if any, payable as a result of this reimbursement. The Association requires that the Executive purchase and be responsible for the maintenance of an automobile for Association business purposes to be housed, for security reasons, at the residence of the Executive; the Association will pay up to $ _____ per month during the period of this Agreement toward that purchase plus all fuel, insurance, and maintenance expenses, with the Executive reimbursing the Association for the cost of any reasonably estimated non-business use of the automobile, including commuting.

  4. *Cancellation*.

  A. The Association may cancel this Agreement: (i) immediately in the event of the death of the Executive; (ii) thirty days after the onset of physical or mental disability, confirmed by a professional medical diagnosis, that prevents the effective performance of the Executive's duties; or (iii) immediately in the event of documented acts of dishonesty, fraud, or gross negligence by the Executive in connection with performance of the Executive's duties to the Association, with those acts disclosed to the Executive, with the Executive accorded an opportunity to respond in writing or in person—at the Executive's option—to the Executive Committee of the Association, with the Executive receiving no further compensation beyond the cancellation date other than benefits accrued or required by law, and with the Association having sole authority for any communications within the Association or to the public regarding the cancellation.

B. The Association may cancel this Agreement for any other reasons, which need not be disclosed to the Executive, by giving the Executive written notice of the cancellation and paying full compensation to the Executive during the notice period; at its sole discretion, the Association will determine whether to require that the Executive perform the Executive's duties for the Association during that notice period; the length of that notice period is one month for each completed year of the Executive's tenure with the Association, subject to a minimum of _____ months and a maximum of _____ months, which period may extend beyond the then-current annual term of this Agreement and the Agreement will automatically be extended through that notice period only; the Association and the Executive will mutually agree upon any communications within the Association or to the public regarding the cancellation.

C. The Executive may cancel this Agreement by giving the Association _____ months' advance notice in writing, with any longer notice subject to the approval of the Executive Committee of the Association; the notice may extend beyond the then-current annual term of this Agreement and the Agreement will automatically be extended through that notice period only. The Executive will receive full compensation during that notice period; at its sole discretion, the Association will determine whether to require that the Executive perform the Executive's duties for the Association during that notice period; the Association and the Executive will mutually agree upon any communications within the Association or to the public regarding the cancellation.

5. *Intellectual Property, Confidentiality, Non-Compete, and Investments*. The Executive recognizes and agrees that all copyrights, trademarks, or other intellectual property rights to created works arising in any way from the Executive's employment by the Association are the sole and exclusive property of the Association and agrees to not assert any such rights against the Association or any third-parties. Upon cancellation of this Agreement by either party for any reason, the Executive will relinquish to the Association all documents, books, manuals, lists, records, publications or other writings, keys, credit cards, equipment, or other articles that came into the Executive's possession in connection with the Executive's employment by the Association and to maintain no copies or duplicates without the written approval of the Executive Committee of the Association. The Executive will maintain in confidence during and subsequent to the Executive's employment any information about the Association or its members which is confidential information or which might reasonably be expected by the Executive to be regarded by the Association or its members as confidential. Upon cancellation of this Agreement by either party for any reason, the Executive will refrain for one year from undertaking employment or any compensated duties on behalf of any association or firm that provides services or products to _____ in competition with the Association unless the Executive Committee of the Association approves the employment or duties in writing. The Executive will not make or direct any personal investments in the _____ field based substantially upon informa-

tion conveyed to the Executive as the _____ of the Association where the information is conveyed with a request for, or in the expectation of, confidentiality.

6. *Indemnification*. The Association indemnifies, holds harmless, and will defend the Executive against claims arising against the Executive in connection with the Executive's performance of the duties of the Executive's employment by the Association to the full extent permitted by law but not with respect to claims successfully resolved against the Executive that the Executive engaged in fraudulent, grossly negligent, criminal, or *ultra vires* acts.

7. *Successors*. This Agreement is binding upon the Association and the Executive, their heirs, executors, administrators, successors, and assigns. The Executive will not assign or designate any part of the Executive's rights or responsibilities under this Agreement unless the Executive Committee of the Association agrees in writing to the assignment or designation. In the event of dissolution of the Association, this Agreement will continue in force through the then-current period of employment. In the event of any merger, consolidation, or reorganization involving the Association, this Agreement becomes an obligation of any legal successor or successors to the Association.

8. *Entire Agreement*. This document contains the entire agreement of the Association and the Executive. It may not be changed orally but only by an agreement in writing signed by the Association and the Executive. This Agreement supersedes and cancels all previous agreements between the Association and the Executive.

9. *Governing Law*. This Agreement is governed by the laws of the State of _____.

Association

_____   By_____
Date

                     Title_____

_____   _____
Date

CHAPTER 12

Professional Development for the Chief Executive Officer

In general, the tenure of a chief executive officer (CEO) ranges from five to eight years. If you become a CEO at 45 years of age, which many do, you may make two or more moves before you retire. So, arriving at the CEO level might not be so much an ending as a beginning. And unless you continue to develop the knowledge, skills, and qualities that propelled you to the top, you might stall there and even be at risk of failing.

Another point to ponder is that your previous positions and your career developed side by side and will continue to do so as you settle into a new assignment. Eventually, you may find that the position is not growing as fast or broadly as you are able and thus you find yourself pushing open the door to other, larger opportunities. Or, your position may expand beyond the ability you initially brought to the association; unless you grow professionally, you may find the executive committee opening the door for you.

These scenarios, among others, result from of a variety of forces. Forces internal to the executive are what make a person want to lead, make decisions, assume risks, solve problems, and make things better. But an association is not a business. You don't own it. While you, as CEO, may influence the measurement criteria, success is determined ultimately by how well the association meets the needs of its members—the people who own it.

External forces are largely determined by others, and you may see them as fixed. For this reason, the excitement of a new position can stall after a few years and, before you know it, you're looking for a new opportunity.

It is possible, however, to come to a stall because you failed to develop the potential of the position you are in; perhaps you did not take the time to seek opportunities to grow professionally and thus keep your job interesting. When you sense a stall, do not automatically look for a new position. Clearly, every job has its limitations, but executives often are too quick to look for change in *where* they work rather than *how* they work and *what* they are currently doing. Professional development does not necessarily mean changing your employer, but it most assuredly means changing you.

As change sweeps through the external environment in which associations operate, they must change as well to remain relevant to members' needs. For the CEO, this means not only learning new ways of doing things—such as reacting to needs and stimulus—but also looking for new ways to act. Your attitude toward change is a good measure of whether you are still growing as a professional. If you find yourself resisting change, putting off suggestions from board members on new product or service lines, ignoring subordinates' recommendations on developing membership or selling exhibit space, watch out. Your association can change or it can be changed—but it cannot remain the same. Neither can you.

On the other hand, if you welcome change and insist on exploring new methods and technologies to achieve and enhance goals, then your value to your current association—and your prospects with other associations—will grow. Associations are service organizations, driven by the people who work in them. To develop better products and services, you need continuous development and training of professionals and other staff. And what better place to start than the executive suite? Search committees respond favorably to CEO candidates committed to and experienced in staff development, and they are particularly attracted to candidates whose resumes indicate a personal commitment to self-improvement and professional growth.

The fact is, in a world of continual and accelerating change, if you are not growing you are shrinking. Period.

Selected Resources

"Finding Wisdom in Fellows' Words," *ASSOCIATION MANAGEMENT*, June 2000, pp. 57–60, American Society of Association Executives, Washington, DC. Full-text available at: http://www.asaenet.org/research/detail/ 0,,50672,00.html

ABSTRACT: New American Society of Association Executives fellows for the year 2000 offer advice for young professionals who are beginning careers in associations, discuss the future of association management, and reflect on changes that have occurred since they began working in the association arena.

Hortum, Leslie W. "Positioning Yourself for the Top Job," *ASSOCIATION MANAGEMENT*, August 2000, pp. 60–62, 64, American Society of Association Executives, Washington, DC. Full-text available at: http://www. asaenet.org/ am/article/1,1057,51027-feature,00.html

ABSTRACT: To be considered for an association chief staff executive position one needs to understand how the association business is changing, how the executive search business has changed, and how best to demonstrate one's abilities in this new environment. Organizations are seeking candidates for chief executive officer (CEO) positions with a strong business focus, an understanding of the association-management profession, and an entrepreneurial spiritas well as an ability to develop creative ways to enhance nondues revenue. The prospective CEO should emphasize broad experience, continual career development, and out-of-the-box thinking.

Kaul, Pamela A. "Pump Up Your Employment Potential," *ASSOCIATION MANAGEMENT*, August 2000, American Society of Association Executives, Washington, DC. Full-text available at: http://www.asaenet.org/am/article/1,1057,51029-feature,00.html

ABSTRACT: Expert advice for getting and staying ready for leadership positions stresses preparation for the job and keeping skills honed. Prospective applicants for promotions or new jobs need to express their unique values succinctly, with examples from past successes, in such a way that interviewers want to hear more. Employers look for transferable skills, like creative problem solving and situational leadership that will meet their specific needs and the corporate culture. Soft skills such as effective communication and listening, consensus building, and teamwork are as important as knowledge sharing and the transfer of best practices. Contenders should be just as aware of what they don't know, especially about finance and information technology. Since CEOs must nurture strategic alliances and maintain a variety of relationships, being politically astute and keeping in touch with staff, competitors, and stakeholders is a must.

Kosko, Jill. "Reevaluate Your Resume," Communication News, August 2000, American Society of Association Executives, Washington, DC. Full-text available at: http://www.asaenet.org/sections/comm/article/1,2261,50971,00.html

ABSTRACT: A resume that works can be put together by being straightforward, explaining promotions and new responsibilities, and addressing gaps in your career. Also, list special accomplishments as well as activities outside of work that will cast you in a positive light, all the while limiting the resume to two pages.

Swanson, Ed. "Targeting the Student Audience," *ASSOCIATION MANAGEMENT*, October 2000, p. 20, American Society of Association Executives, Washington, DC.

ABSTRACT: Video classroom programs for students are one way for associations to reach young people who are beginning to plan careers. To be effective, video programs should be developed with educators and professional video producers so they capture the attention of media-savvy teenagers. Such programs must fit within educational guidelines, fill an educational need, and contain instructor resources.